Ninja Dual Zone Air Fryer

Cookbook for Beginners UK

2000+ Super Easy, Quick and Delicious Recipes Book | Expert Tips for Air Frying, Grilling, and Baking in Less Than 30 Minutes

Leentje Mager

Copyright © 2024 by Leentje Mager

All rights reserved worldwide.

No portion of this work may be reproduced or transmitted in any form or by any means, electronic or mechanical, including photocopying, recording, or any information retrieval system, without the prior written permission of the publisher, except for brief quotations used in critical reviews.

Legal Disclaimer:

This material is protected by copyright law and is intended solely for personal use. Any unauthorized distribution, resale, or utilization of the content contained herein is strictly prohibited and may lead to legal action.

Warning and Disclaimer:

The content presented in this work is provided for educational and entertainment purposes only. While every effort has been made to ensure its accuracy and reliability, no warranties, express or implied, are provided. The author does not offer legal, financial, medical, or professional advice. By accessing this material, the reader acknowledges that the author and publisher are not liable for any direct or indirect losses resulting from the utilization of the information presented herein, including but not limited to errors or omissions.

Furthermore, readers are advised to exercise caution and discretion when applying the concepts discussed in this work to their personal or professional lives. It is recommended to seek guidance from appropriate experts or professionals before making significant decisions based on the contents herein. The author and publisher disclaim any responsibility for any unfavorable outcomes arising from the application of the ideas, recommendations, or strategies outlined in this work.

Table of Contents

Introduction 2

CHAPTER 1 Breakfast Delights 5

CHAPTER 2 Easy Daily Favourites 12

CHAPTER 3 Poultry and Meat 16

CHAPTER 4 Beef, Pork, and Lamb 24

CHAPTER 5 Fish and Seafood 34

CHAPTER 6 Snacks and Starters 41

CHAPTER 7 Vegetables and Sides 47

CHAPTER 8 Vegetarian Mains 53

CHAPTER 9 Treats and Desserts 56

Appendix 1: Recipe Index 59

Introduction

Introducing the culinary sensation: Ninja Dual Zone Air Fryer Cookbook. Get ready to embark on a flavorful voyage that will redefine your kitchen experience and ignite your passion for cooking. Imagine crispy textures, succulent meats, and vibrant vegetables—all without the guilt of excess oil. With the Ninja Dual Zone Air Fryer Cookbook, culinary excellence is within reach like never before.

Prepare to discover a world where innovation meets indulgence, where each recipe is a masterpiece of taste and health. Say farewell to conventional frying methods and embrace a healthier alternative that doesn't compromise on flavor. The Ninja Dual Zone Air Fryer sets the stage for a new era of cooking, delivering the perfect blend of crispiness and succulence in every dish.

Central to our cookbook is the Ninja Dual Zone Air Fryer—an embodiment of culinary brilliance. Its dual cooking zones empower you to multitask effortlessly, allowing you to create a symphony of flavors without the risk of flavor blending. More than just an appliance, it's a culinary companion that elevates every meal to new heights.

But our cookbook is not just a collection of recipes; it's a treasure trove of culinary expertise. Dive into the intricacies of temperature control, uncover the secrets of flavor enhancement through marinades and spices, and master the art of air fryer maintenance for longevity and peak performance.

So, are you prepared to embark on a gastronomic escapade? Let the Ninja's Dual Zone Air Fryer Cookbook be your guide as we navigate the realms of crispy perfection together. From tantalizing starters to decadent desserts, each recipe is a testament to the limitless possibilities of air frying. Embrace the culinary revolution and join us on a journey to epicurean delight.

Air frying is revolutionizing the way we approach cooking, offering a healthier alternative to traditional frying methods while retaining the delicious flavors and textures we love. Here's why air frying, especially with the Ninja Dual Zone Air Fryer, is gaining momentum:

Healthier Cooking: By using hot air circulation instead of oil, air frying significantly reduces the amount of fat and calories in dishes. Enjoy guilt-free indulgence with crispy results and minimal oil, perfect for those seeking a healthier lifestyle.

Culinary Versatility: The Ninja Dual Zone Air Fryer isn't limited to frying—it's a culinary powerhouse capable of grilling, roasting, and baking. From golden fries to succulent meats and beyond, explore a world of culinary possibilities with this versatile appliance.

Time-Efficient Convenience: With its rapid hot air circulation, the Ninja Dual Zone Air Fryer cooks food faster than conventional methods. Say goodbye to lengthy cooking times and hello to quick and convenient meals, ideal for busy individuals and families.

Precision Cooking Control: Featuring dual cooking zones and precise temperature control, the Ninja Dual Zone Air Fryer ensures consistent results with every use. Whether you're cooking multiple dishes at once or experimenting with new recipes, you can trust in precise and reliable performance.

Effortless Cleanup: Cleaning up after cooking is effortless with the Ninja Dual Zone Air Fryer. Its non-stick surfaces and dishwasher-safe components make post-cooking cleanup a breeze, allowing you to spend less time scrubbing and more time enjoying your culinary creations.

Space-Saving Design: Despite its impressive capabilities, the Ninja Dual Zone Air Fryer boasts a sleek and compact design that won't clutter your kitchen countertops. Its modern aesthetic seamlessly integrates into any kitchen space, enhancing both form and function.

Tips for Getting Started with the Ninja Dual Zone Air Fryer:

Step 1: Unbox and Familiarize: Begin by unpacking your Ninja Dual Zone Air Fryer and acquainting yourself with its components. Take a moment to peruse the instruction manual thoroughly, ensuring you understand its functionality and features.

Step 2: Choose an Ideal Location: Select a suitable spot for your air fryer, ensuring it's placed on a stable, flat surface with ample ventilation. Position it away from walls and other appliances to allow proper airflow.

Step 3: Preheat the Air Fryer: Preheating your air fryer is crucial for achieving optimal cooking results. Refer to the manual for specific preheating instructions based on your recipe or desired cooking temperature.

Step 4: Select Cooking Zones: Decide whether you'll utilize both cooking zones or just one based on your cooking needs. The flexibility of the Ninja Dual Zone Air Fryer allows you to cook different dishes simultaneously, maximizing efficiency.

Step 5: Load the Food: Place your desired ingredients into the cooking baskets or on the crisper plates. Utilize the dual cooking zones to prepare dishes with varying cooking times or temperature requirements.

Step 6: Set Time and Temperature: Utilize the intuitive control panel to set the cooking time and temperature according to your recipe. Enjoy precise control over your cooking process, ensuring perfectly cooked meals every time.

Step 7: Initiate Cooking: Once you've inputted your desired settings, initiate the cooking process by pressing the start button. Sit back and relax as the air fryer circulates hot air around your food, delivering even and consistent cooking.

Step 8: Monitor Progress: Keep an eye on the cooking progress through the transparent viewing window or by cautiously opening the air fryer. Consider flipping or shaking the food midway through cooking for uniform browning.

Step 9: Check for Doneness: Use a food thermometer or visually inspect the food to determine if it's cooked to your liking. Adjust the cooking time or temperature as needed to achieve your desired level of doneness.

Step 10: Serve and Enjoy: Once your culinary creations are ready, carefully remove them from the air fryer and serve immediately. Delight in the crispy, flavorful results of your efforts!

Step 11: Cleaning and Maintenance: After each use, ensure the air fryer is unplugged and allowed to cool down. Clean removable parts with warm, soapy water or place them in the dishwasher for effortless maintenance. Wipe the exterior of the air fryer with a damp cloth to keep it looking pristine.

By following these steps, you'll unlock the full potential of your Ninja Dual Zone Air Fryer and embark on a culinary journey filled with delicious and healthier meals!

Maintaining Your Ninja Dual Zone Air Fryer:

Start with Safety: Before diving into the cleaning process, ensure your Ninja Dual Zone Air Fryer is unplugged and has cooled down completely to prevent any accidents or injuries.

Disassemble with Care: Take apart all removable components of your air fryer, such as the cooking baskets, trays, and accessories. Handle each piece gently to avoid any damage.

Gentle Cleansing Ritual: Wash the removable parts with warm, soapy water using a soft sponge or cloth. For stubborn stains, a mild solution of baking soda and water can work wonders without damaging the surfaces.

Mindful Interior Maintenance: Using a damp cloth or sponge, carefully wipe down the interior of your air fryer, paying special attention to areas prone to grease buildup. Avoid harsh scrubbing to preserve the non-stick coating.

Delicate Heating Element TLC: With caution, clean the heating element by gently wiping it down with a damp cloth. Take care not to apply excessive pressure, as this component is sensitive and critical to the air fryer's function.

Exterior Elegance: Restore the exterior of your air fryer to its pristine state by wiping it down with a cloth or sponge dampened with mild dish soap. Be thorough in removing any grease or residue for a polished finish.

Thorough Drying and Reassembly: Ensure all components are completely dry before reassembling your air fryer. Any lingering moisture could lead to mold or deterioration. Once dry, carefully put everything back together.

Protective Measures: Consider using silicone liners or reusable air fryer mats to protect the non-stick surfaces of your air fryer and simplify cleanup. These accessories can extend the lifespan of your appliance while minimizing mess.

By incorporating these gentle cleaning practices into your routine, you can ensure your Ninja Dual Zone Air Fryer remains in optimal condition, ready to whip up delicious and healthy meals with ease.

CHAPTER 1 Breakfast Delights

Bunless Breakfast Turkey Burgers

Prep time: 5 minutes | Cook time: 15 minutes | Serves 4

- 450 g turkey banger meat, removed from casings
- ½ teaspoon salt
- ¼ teaspoon ground black pepper
- 60 g seeded and chopped green pepper
- 2 tablespoons mayonnaise
- 1 medium avocado, peeled, pitted, and sliced

1. In a large bowl, mix banger meat with salt, black pepper, pepper, and mayonnaise. Form meat into four patties. 2. Place patties into ungreased air fryer basket. Adjust the temperature to 190°C and air fry for 15 minutes, turning patties halfway through cooking. Burgers will be done when dark brown and they have an internal temperature of at least 74°C. 3. Serve burgers topped with avocado slices on four medium plates.

Cheddar Eggs

Prep time: 5 minutes | Cook time: 15 minutes | Serves 2

- 4 large eggs
- 2 tablespoons unsalted butter, melted
- 120 g grated mature Cheddar cheese

1. Crack eggs into a round baking dish and whisk. Place dish into the air fryer basket. 2. Adjust the temperature to 200°C and set the timer for 10 minutes. 3. After 5 minutes, stir the eggs and add the butter and cheese. Let cook 3 more minutes and stir again. 4. Allow eggs to finish cooking an additional 2 minutes or remove if they are to your desired liking. 5. Use a fork to fluff. Serve warm.

Not-So-English Muffins

Prep time: 5 minutes | Cook time: 10 minutes | Serves 4

- 2 strips turkey bacon, cut in half crosswise
- 2 whole-grain English muffins, split
- 235 ml fresh baby spinach, long stems removed
- ¼ ripe pear, peeled and thinly sliced
- 4 slices low-moisture Mozzarella or other melting cheese

1. Place bacon strips in air fryer basket and air fry at 200°C for 2 minutes. Check and separate strips if necessary so they cook evenly. Cook for 3 to 4 more minutes, until crispy. Remove and drain on paper towels. 2. Place split muffin halves in air fryer basket and cook for 2 minutes, just until lightly browned. 3. Open air fryer and top each muffin with a quarter of the baby spinach, several pear slices, a strip of bacon, and a slice of cheese. 4. Air fry at 182°C for 1 to 2 minutes, until cheese completely melts.

Cheesy Scrambled Eggs

Prep time: 2 minutes | Cook time: 9 minutes | Serves 2

- 1 teaspoon unsalted butter
- 2 large eggs
- 2 tablespoons milk
- 2 tablespoons grated Cheddar cheese
- Salt and freshly ground black pepper, to taste

1. Preheat the air fryer to 150°C. Place the butter in a baking pan and cook for 1 to 2 minutes, until melted. 2. In a small bowl, whisk together the eggs, milk, and cheese. Season with salt and black pepper. Transfer the mixture to the pan. 3. Cook for 3 minutes. Stir the eggs and push them toward themaize center of the pan. 4. Cook for another 2 minutes, then stir again. Cook for another 2 minutes, until the eggs are just cooked. Serve warm.

Spinach and Bacon Roll-ups

Prep time: 5 minutes | Cook time: 8 to 9 minutes | Serves 4

- 4 wheat maize wraps (6- or 7-inch size)
- 4 slices Swiss cheese
- 235 g baby spinach leaves
- 4 slices turkey bacon
- Special Equipment:
- 4 cocktail sticks, soak in water for at least 30 minutes

1. Preheat the air fryer to 200°C. 2. On a clean work surface, top each tortilla with one slice of cheese and 60 ml spinach, then tightly roll them up. 3. Wrap each tortilla with a strip of turkey bacon and secure with a toothpick. 4. Arrange the

roll-ups in the air fryer basket, leaving space between each roll-up. 5. Air fry for 4 minutes. Flip the roll-ups with tongs and rearrange them for more even cooking. Air fry for another 4 to 5 minutes until the bacon is crisp. 6. Rest for 5 minutes and remove the cocktail sticks before serving.

Breakfast Pitta

Prep time: 5 minutes | Cook time: 6 minutes | Serves 2

- 1 wholemeal pitta
- 2 teaspoons rapeseed oil
- ½ shallot, diced
- ¼ teaspoon garlic, minced
- 1 large egg
- ¼ teaspoon dried oregano
- ¼ teaspoon dried thyme
- ⅛ teaspoon salt
- 2 tablespoons grated Parmesan cheese

1. Preheat the air fryer to 190°C. 2. Brush the top of the pitta with rapeseed oil, then spread the diced shallot and minced garlic over the pitta. 3. Crack the egg into a small bowl or ramekin, and season it with oregano, thyme, and salt. 4. Place the pitta into the air fryer basket, and gently pour the egg onto the top of the pitta. Sprinkle with cheese over the top. 5. Bake for 6 minutes. 6. Allow to cool for 5 minutes before cutting into pieces for serving.

Bourbon Vanilla Eggy Bread

Prep time: 15 minutes | Cook time: 6 minutes | Serves 4

- 2 large eggs
- 2 tablespoons water
- 160 ml whole or semi-skimmed milk
- 1 tablespoon butter, melted
- 2 tablespoons bourbon
- 1 teaspoon vanilla extract
- 8 (1-inch-thick) French bread slices
- Cooking spray

1. Preheat the air fryer to 160°C. Line the air fryer basket with parchment paper and spray it with cooking spray. 2. Beat the eggs with the water in a shallow bowl until combined. Add the milk, melted butter, bourbon, and vanilla and stir to mix well. 3. Dredge 4 slices of bread in the batter, turning to coat both sides evenly. Transfer the bread slices onto the parchment paper. 4. Bake for 6 minutes until nicely browned. Flip the slices halfway through the cooking time. 5. Remove from the basket to a plate and repeat with the remaining 4 slices of bread. 6. Serve warm.

Pancake for Two

Prep time: 5 minutes | Cook time: 30 minutes | Serves 2

- 120 g blanched finely ground almond flour
- 2 tablespoons granular erythritol
- 1 tablespoon salted butter, melted
- 1 large egg
- 80 ml unsweetened almond milk
- ½ teaspoon vanilla extract

1. In a large bowl, mix all ingredients together, then pour half the batter into an ungreased round nonstick baking dish. 2. Place dish into air fryer basket. Adjust the temperature to 160°C and bake for 15 minutes. The pancake will be golden brown on top and firm, and a toothpick inserted in the center will come out clean when done. Repeat with remaining batter. 3. Slice in half in dish and serve warm.

Asparagus and Pepper Strata

Prep time: 10 minutes | Cook time: 14 to 20 minutes | Serves 4

- 8 large asparagus spears, trimmed and cut into 2-inch pieces
- 80 g grated carrot
- 120 g chopped red pepper
- 2 slices wholemeal bread, cut into ½-inch cubes
- 3 egg whites
- 1 egg
- 3 tablespoons 1% milk
- ½ teaspoon dried thyme

1. In a baking pan, combine the asparagus, carrot, red pepper, and 1 tablespoon of water. Bake in the air fryer at 170°C for 3 to 5 minutes, or until crisp-tender. Drain well. 2. Add the bread cubes to the vegetables and gently toss. 3. In a medium bowl, whisk the egg whites, egg, milk, and thyme until frothy. 4. Pour the egg mixture into the pan. Bake for 11 to 15 minutes, or until the strata is slightly puffy and set and the top starts to brown. Serve.

Lemon-Blueberry Muffins

Prep time: 5 minutes | Cook time: 20 to 25 minutes | Makes 6 muffins

- 150 g almond flour
- 3 tablespoons granulated sweetener
- 1 teaspoon baking powder

- 2 large eggs
- 3 tablespoons melted butter
- 1 tablespoon almond milk
- 1 tablespoon fresh lemon juice
- 120 g fresh blueberries

1. Preheat the air fryer to 180°C. Lightly coat 6 silicone muffin cups with vegetable oil. Set aside. 2. In a large mixing bowl, combine the almond flour, sweetener, and baking soda. Set aside. 3. In a separate small bowl, whisk together the eggs, butter, milk, and lemon juice. Add the egg mixture to the flour mixture and stir until just combined. Fold in the blueberries and let the batter sit for 5 minutes. 4. Spoon the muffin batter into the muffin cups, about two-thirds full. Air fry for 20 to 25 minutes, or until a toothpick inserted into the center of a muffin comes out clean. 5. Remove the basket from the air fryer and let the muffins cool for about 5 minutes before transferring them to a wire rack to cool completely.

Scotch Eggs

Prep time: 10 minutes | Cook time: 20 to 25 minutes | Serves 4

- 2 tablespoons flour, plus extra for coating
- 450 g banger meat
- 4 hard-boiled eggs, peeled
- 1 raw egg
- 1 tablespoon water
- Oil for misting or cooking spray
- Crumb Coating:
- 90 g breadcrumbs
- 90 g flour

1. Combine flour with banger meat and mix thoroughly. 2. Divide into 4 equal portions and mould each around a hard-boiled egg so the banger completely covers the egg. 3. In a small bowl, beat together the raw egg and water. 4. Dip banger-covered eggs in the remaining flour, then the egg mixture, then roll in the crumb coating. 5. Air fry at 180°C for 10 minutes. Spray eggs, turn, and spray other side. 6. Continue cooking for another 10 to 15 minutes or until banger is well done.

Cauliflower Avocado Toast

Prep time: 15 minutes | Cook time: 8 minutes | Serves 2

- 1 (40 g) steamer bag cauliflower
- 1 large egg
- 120 g grated Cheddar cheese
- 1 ripe medium avocado
- ½ teaspoon garlic powder
- ¼ teaspoon ground black pepper

1. Cook cauliflower according to package instructions. Remove from bag and place into cheesecloth or clean towel to remove excess moisture. 2. Place cauliflower into a large bowl and mix in egg and Mozzarella. Cut a piece of parchment to fit your air fryer basket. Separate the cauliflower mixture into two, and place it on the parchment in two mounds. Press out the cauliflower mounds into a ¼-inch-thick rectangle. Place the parchment into the air fryer basket. 3. Adjust the temperature to 200°C and set the timer for 8 minutes. 4. Flip the cauliflower halfway through the cooking time. 5. When the timer beeps, remove the parchment and allow the cauliflower to cool 5 minutes. 6. Cut open the avocado and remove the pit. Scoop out the inside, place it in a medium bowl, and mash it with garlic powder and pepper. Spread onto the cauliflower. Serve immediately.

Western Frittata

Prep time: 10 minutes | Cook time: 19 minutes | Serves 1 to 2

- ½ red or green pepper, cut into ½-inch chunks
- 1 teaspoon rapeseed oil
- 3 eggs, beaten
- 60 g grated Cheddar cheese
- 60 g diced cooked gammon
- Salt and freshly ground black pepper, to taste
- 1 teaspoon butter
- 1 teaspoon chopped fresh parsley

1. Preheat the air fryer to 200°C. 2. Toss the peppers with the rapeseed oil and air fry for 6 minutes, shaking the basket once or twice during the cooking process to redistribute the ingredients. 3. While the vegetables are cooking, beat the eggs well in a bowl, stir in the Cheddar cheese and gammon, and season with salt and freshly ground black pepper. Add the air-fried peppers to this bowl when they have finished cooking. 4. Place a cake pan into the air fryer basket with the butter using an aluminum sling to lower the pan into the basket. Air fry for 1 minute at 190°C to melt the butter. Remove the cake pan and rotate the pan to distribute the butter and grease the pan. Pour the egg mixture into the cake pan and return the pan to the air fryer, using the aluminum sling. 5. Air fry at 190°C for

12 minutes, or until the frittata has puffed up and is lightly browned. Let the frittata sit in the air fryer for 5 minutes to cool to an edible temperature and set up. Remove the cake pan from the air fryer, sprinkle with parsley and serve immediately.

Baked Potato Breakfast Boats

Prep time: 10 minutes | Cook time: 20 minutes | Serves 4

- 2 large white potatoes, scrubbed
- rapeseed oil
- Salt and freshly ground black pepper, to taste
- 4 eggs
- 2 tablespoons chopped, cooked bacon
- 235 g grated Cheddar cheese

1. Poke holes in the potatoes with a fork and microwave on full power for 5 minutes. 2. Turn potatoes over and cook an additional 3 to 5 minutes, or until the potatoes are fork-tender. 3. Cut the potatoes in half lengthwise and use a spoon to scoop out the inside of the potato. Be careful to leave a layer of potato so that it makes a sturdy "boat." 4. Preheat the air fryer to 180°C. 5. Lightly spray the air fryer basket with rapeseed oil. Spray the skin side of the potatoes with oil and sprinkle with salt and pepper to taste. 6. Place the potato skins in the air fryer basket, skin-side down. Crack one egg into each potato skin. 7. Sprinkle ½ tablespoon of bacon pieces and 60 ml grated cheese on top of each egg. Sprinkle with salt and pepper to taste. 8. Air fry until the yolk is slightly runny, 5 to 6 minutes, or until the yolk is fully cooked, 7 to 10 minutes.

Portobello Eggs Benedict

Prep time: 10 minutes | Cook time: 10 to 14 minutes | Serves 2

- 1 tablespoon rapeseed oil
- 2 cloves garlic, minced
- ¼ teaspoon dried thyme
- 2 portobello mushrooms, stems removed and gills scraped out
- 2 vine tomatoes, halved lengthwise
- Salt and freshly ground black pepper, to taste
- 2 large eggs
- 2 tablespoons grated Pecorino Romano cheese
- 1 tablespoon chopped fresh parsley, for garnish
- 1 teaspoon truffle oil (optional)

1. Preheat the air fryer to 200°C. 2. In a small bowl, combine the rapeseed oil, garlic, and thyme. Brush the mixture over the mushrooms and tomatoes until thoroughly coated. Season to taste with salt and freshly ground black pepper. 3. Arrange the vegetables, cut side up, in the air fryer basket. Crack an egg into the center of each mushroom and sprinkle with cheese. Air fry for 10 to 14 minutes until the vegetables are tender and the whites are firm. When cool enough to handle, coarsely chop the tomatoes and place on top of the eggs. Scatter parsley on top and drizzle with truffle oil, if desired, just before serving.

Quesadillas

Prep time: 10 minutes | Cook time: 15 minutes | Serves 4

- 4 eggs
- 2 tablespoons skimmed milk
- Salt and pepper, to taste
- Oil for misting or cooking spray
- 4 wheat maize wraps
- 4 tablespoons tomato salsa
- 60 g Cheddar cheese, grated
- ½ small avocado, peeled and thinly sliced

1. Preheat the air fryer to 130°C. 2. Beat together eggs, milk, salt, and pepper. 3. Spray a baking pan lightly with cooking spray and add egg mixture. 4. Bake for 8 to 9 minutes, stirring every 1 to 2 minutes, until eggs are scrambled to your liking. Remove and set aside. 5. Spray one side of each maize wrap with oil or cooking spray. Flip over. 6. Divide eggs, tomato salsa, cheese, and avocado among the maize wraps, covering only half of each maize wrap. 7. Fold each maize wrap in half and press down lightly. 8. Place 2 maize wraps in air fryer basket and air fry at 200°C for 3 minutes or until cheese melts and outside feels slightly crispy. Repeat with remaining two maize wraps. 9. Cut each cooked maize wrap into halves or thirds.

Cinnamon-Raisin Bagels

Prep time: 30 minutes | Cook time: 10 minutes | Makes 4 bagels

- Oil, for spraying
- 60 g raisins
- 120 g self-raising flour, plus more for dusting
- 235 ml natural yoghurt
- 1 teaspoon ground cinnamon
- 1 large egg

1. Line the air fryer basket with parchment and spray lightly with oil. 2. Place the raisins in a bowl of hot water and let sit for 10 to 15 minutes, until they have plumped. This will make them

extra juicy. 3. In a large bowl, mix together the flour, yoghurt, and cinnamon with your hands or a large silicone spatula until a ball is formed. It will be quite sticky for a while. 4. Drain the raisins and gently work them into the ball of dough. 5. Place the dough on a lightly floured work surface and divide into 4 equal pieces. Roll each piece into an 8- or 9-inch-long rope and shape it into a circle, pinching the ends together to seal. 6. In a small bowl, whisk the egg. Brush the egg onto the tops of the dough. 7. Place the dough in the prepared basket. 8. Air fry at 180°C for 10 minutes. Serve immediately.

Cinnamon Rolls

Prep time: 10 minutes | Cook time: 20 minutes | Makes 12 rolls

- 600 g grated Cheddar cheese
- 60 g soft cheese, softened
- 120 g blanched finely ground almond flour
- ½ teaspoon vanilla extract
- 96 ml icing sugar-style sweetener
- 1 tablespoon ground cinnamon

1. In a large microwave-safe bowl, combine Cheddar cheese, soft cheese, and flour. Microwave the mixture on high 90 seconds until cheese is melted. 2. Add vanilla extract and sweetener, and mix 2 minutes until a dough forms. 3. Once the dough is cool enough to work with your hands, about 2 minutes, spread it out into a 12 × 4-inch rectangle on ungreased parchment paper. Evenly sprinkle dough with cinnamon. 4. Starting at the long side of the dough, roll lengthwise to form a log. Slice the log into twelve even pieces. 5. Divide rolls between two ungreased round nonstick baking dishes. Place one dish into air fryer basket. Adjust the temperature to 190°C and bake for 10 minutes. 6. Cinnamon rolls will be done when golden around the edges and mostly firm. Repeat with second dish. Allow rolls to cool in dishes 10 minutes before serving.

Simple Cinnamon Toasts

Prep time: 5 minutes | Cook time: 4 minutes | Serves 4

- 1 tablespoon salted butter
- 2 teaspoons ground cinnamon
- 4 tablespoons sugar
- ½ teaspoon vanilla extract
- 10 bread slices

1. Preheat the air fryer to 190°C. 2. In a bowl, combine the butter, cinnamon, sugar, and vanilla extract. Spread onto the slices of bread. 3. Put the bread inside the air fryer and bake for 4 minutes or until golden brown. 4. Serve warm.

Bacon, Egg, and Cheese Roll Ups

Prep time: 15 minutes | Cook time: 15 minutes | Serves 4

- 2 tablespoons unsalted butter
- 60 g chopped onion
- ½ medium green pepper, seeded and chopped
- 6 large eggs
- 12 slices bacon
- 235 g grated mature Cheddar cheese
- 120 ml mild tomato salsa, for dipping

1. In a medium frying pan over medium heat, melt butter. Add onion and pepper to the frying pan and sauté until fragrant and onions are translucent, about 3 minutes. 2. Whisk eggs in a small bowl and pour into frying pan. Scramble eggs with onions and peppers until fluffy and fully cooked, about 5 minutes. Remove from heat and set aside. 3. On work surface, place three slices of bacon side by side, overlapping about ¼ inch. Place 60 ml scrambled eggs in a heap on the side closest to you and sprinkle 60 ml cheese on top of the eggs. 4. Tightly roll the bacon around the eggs and secure the seam with a toothpick if necessary. Place each roll into the air fryer basket. 5. Adjust the temperature to 180°C and air fry for 15 minutes. Rotate the rolls halfway through the cooking time. 6. Bacon will be brown and crispy when completely cooked. Serve immediately with tomato salsa for dipping.

Breakfast Cobbler

Prep time: 20 minutes | Cook time: 30 minutes | Serves 4

- Filling:
- 280 g banger meat, crumbled
- 60 g minced onions
- 2 cloves garlic, minced
- ½ teaspoon fine sea salt
- ½ teaspoon ground black pepper
- 1 (230 g) package soft cheese (or soft cheese style spread for dairy-free), softened
- 180 g beef or chicken stock
- Biscuits:
- 3 large egg whites
- 90 g blanched almond flour
- 1 teaspoon baking powder
- ¼ teaspoon fine sea salt

- 2½ tablespoons very cold unsalted butter, cut into ¼-inch pieces
- Fresh thyme leaves, for garnish

1. Preheat the air fryer to 200°C. 2. Place the banger, onions, and garlic in a pie dish. Using your hands, break up the banger into small pieces and spread it evenly throughout the pie dish. Season with the salt and pepper. Place the pan in the air fryer and bake for 5 minutes. 3. While the banger cooks, place the soft cheese and stock in a food processor or blender and purée until smooth. 4. Remove the pork from the air fryer and use a fork or metal spatula to crumble it more. Pour the soft cheese mixture into the banger and stir to combine. Set aside. 5. Make the biscuits: Place the egg whites in a medium-sized mixing bowl or the bowl of a stand mixer and whip with a hand mixer or stand mixer until stiff peaks form. 6. In a separate medium-sized bowl, whisk together the almond flour, baking powder, and salt, then cut in the butter. When you are done, the mixture should still have chunks of butter. Gently fold the flour mixture into the egg whites with a rubber spatula. 7. Use a large spoon or ice cream scoop to scoop the dough into 4 equal-sized biscuits, making sure the butter is evenly distributed. Place the biscuits on top of the banger and cook in the air fryer for 5 minutes, then turn the heat down to 160°C and bake for another 17 to 20 minutes, until the biscuits are golden brown. Serve garnished with fresh thyme leaves. 8. Store leftovers in an airtight container in the refrigerator for up to 3 days. Reheat in a preheated 180°C air fryer for 5 minutes, or until warmed through.

Homemade Toaster Pastries

Prep time: 10 minutes | Cook time: 11 minutes | Makes 6 pastries

- Oil, for spraying
- 1 (425 g) package ready-to-roll pie crust
- 6 tablespoons jam or preserves of choice
- 340 g icing sugar
- 3 tablespoons milk
- 1 to 2 tablespoons sprinkles of choice

1. Preheat the air fryer to 180°C. Line the air fryer basket with parchment and lightly spray with oil. 2. Cut the pie crust into 12 rectangles, about 3 by 4 inches each. You will need to reroll the dough scraps to get 12 rectangles. 3. Spread 1 tablespoon of jam in the centre of 6 rectangles, leaving ¼ inch around the edges. 4. Pour some water into a small bowl. Use your finger to moisten the edge of each rectangle. 5. Top each rectangle with another and use your fingers to press around the edges. Using the prongs of a fork, seal the edges of the dough and poke a few holes in the top of each one. Place the pastries in the prepared basket. 6. Air fry for 11 minutes. Let cool completely. 7. In a medium bowl, whisk together the icing sugar and milk. Spread the icing over the tops of the pastries and add sprinkles. Serve immediately.

Jalapeño Popper Egg Cups

Prep time: 10 minutes | Cook time: 10 minutes | Serves 2

- 4 large eggs
- 60 g chopped pickled jalapeños
- 60 g full-fat soft cheese
- 120 g grated mature Cheddar cheese

1. In a medium bowl, beat the eggs, then pour into four silicone muffin cups. 2. In a large microwave-safe bowl, place jalapeños, soft cheese, and Cheddar. Microwave for 30 seconds and stir. Take a spoonful, approximately ¼ of the mixture, and place it in the center of one of the egg cups. Repeat with remaining mixture. 3. Place egg cups into the air fryer basket. 4. Adjust the temperature to 160°C and bake for 10 minutes. 5. Serve warm.

Fried Chicken Wings with Waffles

Prep time: 10 minutes | Cook time: 30 minutes | Serves 4

- 8 whole chicken wings
- 1 teaspoon garlic powder
- Chicken seasoning, for preparing the chicken
- Freshly ground black pepper, to taste
- 60 g plain flour
- Cooking oil spray
- 8 frozen waffles
- Pure maple syrup, for serving (optional)

1. In a medium bowl, combine the chicken and garlic powder and season with chicken seasoning and pepper. Toss to coat. 2. Transfer the chicken to a resealable plastic bag and add the flour. Seal the bag and shake it to coat the chicken thoroughly. 3. Insert the crisper plate into the basket and the basket into the unit. Preheat the unit by selecting AIR FRY, setting the temperature to 200°C, and setting the time to 3 minutes. Select START/STOP to begin. 4. Once the unit is preheated, spray the crisper plate with cooking oil. Using tongs, transfer the chicken from the bag to the basket. It is okay to stack the chicken wings

on top of each other. Spray them with cooking oil. 5. Select AIR FRY, set the temperature to 200ºC, and set the time to 20 minutes. Select START/STOP to begin. 6. After 5 minutes, remove the basket and shake the wings. Reinsert the basket to resume cooking. Remove and shake the basket every 5 minutes until the chicken is fully cooked. 7. When the cooking is complete, remove the cooked chicken from the basket; cover to keep warm. 8. Rinse the basket and crisper plate with warm water. Insert them back into the unit. 9. Select AIR FRY, set the temperature to 180ºC, and set the time to 3 minutes. Select START/STOP to begin. 10. Once the unit is preheated, spray the crisper plate with cooking spray. Working in batches, place the frozen waffles into the basket. Do not stack them. Spray the waffles with cooking oil. 11. Select AIR FRY, set the temperature to 180ºC, and set the time to 6 minutes. Select START/STOP to begin. 12. When the cooking is complete, repeat steps 10 and 11 with the remaining waffles. 13. Serve the waffles with the chicken and a touch of maple syrup, if desired.

Hearty Blueberry Porridge

Prep time: 10 minutes | Cook time: 25 minutes | Serves 6

- 350 g porridge oats
- 1¼ teaspoons ground cinnamon, divided
- ½ teaspoon baking powder
- Pinch salt
- 235 ml unsweetened vanilla almond milk
- 60 ml honey
- 1 teaspoon vanilla extract
- 1 egg, beaten
- 475 g blueberries
- vegetable oil (such as rapeseed oil)
- 1½ teaspoons sugar, divided
- 6 tablespoons low-fat whipped topping (optional)

1. In a large bowl, mix together the oats, 1 teaspoon of cinnamon, baking powder, and salt. 2. In a medium bowl, whisk together the almond milk, honey, vanilla and egg. 3. Pour the liquid ingredients into the oats mixture and stir to combine. Fold in the blueberries. 4. Lightly spray a baking pan with oil. 5. Add half the blueberry mixture to the pan. 6. Sprinkle ⅛ teaspoon of cinnamon and ½ teaspoon sugar over the top. 7. Cover the pan with aluminium foil and place gently in the air fryer basket. 8. Air fry at 180ºC for 20 minutes. Remove the foil and air fry for an additional 5 minutes. Transfer the mixture to a shallow bowl. 9. Repeat with the remaining blueberry mixture, ½ teaspoon of sugar, and ⅛ teaspoon of cinnamon. 10. To serve, spoon into bowls and top with whipped topping.

Oat and Chia Porridge

Prep time: 10 minutes | Cook time: 5 minutes | Serves 4

- 2 tablespoons peanut butter
- 4 tablespoons honey
- 1 tablespoon butter, melted
- 1 L milk
- 475 g oats
- 235 g chia seeds

1. Preheat the air fryer to 200ºC. 2. Put the peanut butter, honey, butter, and milk in a bowl and stir to mix. Add the oats and chia seeds and stir. 3. Transfer the mixture to a bowl and bake in the air fryer for 5 minutes. Give another stir before serving.

CHAPTER 2 Easy Daily Favourites

Bacon-Wrapped Hot Dogs

Prep time: 5 minutes | Cook time: 10 minutes | Serves 4

- Oil, for spraying
- 4 bacon rashers
- 4 hot dog bangers
- 4 hot dog rolls
- Toppings of choice

1. Line the air fryer basket with parchment and spray lightly with oil. 2.Wrap a strip of bacon tightly around each hot dog, taking care to cover the tips so they don't get too crispy. 3.Secure with a toothpick at each end to keep the bacon from shrinking. 4.Place the hot dogs in the prepared basket. 5.Air fry at 190°C for 8 to 9 minutes, depending on how crispy you like the bacon. For extra-crispy, cook the hot dogs at 200°C for 6 to 8 minutes. 6.Place the hot dogs in the buns, return them to the air fryer, and cook for another 1 to 2 minutes, or until the buns are warm. 7.Add your desired toppings and serve.

Pork Burgers with Red Cabbage Salad

Prep time: 20 minutes | Cook time: 7 to 9 minutes | Serves 4

- 120 ml Greek yoghurt
- 2 tablespoons low-salt mustard, divided
- 1 tablespoon lemon juice
- 60 g sliced red cabbage
- 60 g grated carrots
- 450 g lean finely chopped pork
- ½ teaspoon paprika
- 235 g mixed salad leaves
- 2 small tomatoes, sliced
- 8 small low-salt wholemeal sandwich buns, cut in half

1. In a small bowl, combine the yoghurt, 1 tablespoon mustard, lemon juice, cabbage, and carrots; mix and refrigerate. 2.In a medium bowl, combine the pork, remaining 1 tablespoon mustard, and paprika. Form into 8 small patties. Put the sliders into the air fryer basket. 3.Air fry at 200°C for 7 to 9 minutes, or until the sliders register 74°C as tested with a meat thermometer. 4.Assemble the burgers by placing some of the lettuce greens on a bun bottom. 5.Top with a tomato slice, the burgers, and the cabbage mixture. 6.Add the bun top and serve immediately.

Apple Pie Egg Rolls

Prep time: 10 minutes | Cook time: 8 minutes | Makes 6 rolls

- Oil, for spraying
- 1 (600 g) tin apple pie filling
- 1 tablespoon plain flour
- ½ teaspoon lemon juice
- ¼ teaspoon ground nutmeg
- ¼ teaspoon ground cinnamon
- 6 egg roll wrappers

1. Preheat the air fryer to 200°C. 2.Line the air fryer basket with parchment and spray lightly with oil. 3.In a medium bowl, mix together the pie filling, flour, lemon juice, nutmeg, and cinnamon. 4.Lay out the egg roll wrappers on a work surface and spoon a dollop of pie filling in the centre of each. 5.Fill a small bowl with water. Dip your finger in the water and, working one at a time, moisten the edges of the wrappers. 6.Fold the wrapper like an packet: First fold one corner into the centre. 7.Fold each side corner in, and then fold over the remaining corner, making sure each corner overlaps a bit and the moistened edges stay closed. 8.Use additional water and your fingers to seal any open edges. 9.Place the rolls in the prepared basket and spray liberally with oil. 10.You may need to work in batches, depending on the size of your air fryer. 11.Cook for 4 minutes, flip, spray with oil, and cook for another 4 minutes, or until crispy and golden brown. 12.Serve immediately.

Berry Cheese cake

Prep time: 5 minutes | Cook time: 10 minutes | Serves 4

- Oil, for spraying
- 227 g soft white cheese
- 6 tablespoons sugar
- 1 tablespoon sour cream
- 1 large egg
- ½ teaspoon vanilla extract

- ¼ teaspoon lemon juice
- 120 g fresh mixed berries

1. Preheat the air fryer to 180°C. 2.Line the air fryer basket with parchment and spray lightly with oil. 3.In a blender, combine the soft white cheese, sugar, sour cream, egg, vanilla, and lemon juice and blend until smooth. 4.Pour the mixture into a 4-inch springform pan. 5.Place the pan in the prepared basket. Cook for 8 to 10 minutes, or until only the very centre jiggles slightly when the pan is moved. 6.Refrigerate the cheesecake in the pan for at least 2 hours. 7.Release the sides from the springform pan, top the cheesecake with the mixed berries, and serve.

Steak and Vegetable Kebabs

Prep time: 15 minutes | Cook time: 5 to 7 minutes | Serves 4

- 2 tablespoons balsamic vinegar
- 2 teaspoons olive oil
- ½ teaspoon dried marjoram
- ⅛ teaspoon ground black pepper
- 340 g silverside, cut into 1-inch pieces
- 1 red pepper, sliced
- 16 button mushrooms
- 235 g cherry tomatoes

1. In a medium bowl, stir together the balsamic vinegar, olive oil, marjoram, and black pepper. 2.Add the steak and stir to coat. Let stand for 10 minutes at room temperature. 3.Alternating items, thread the beef, red pepper, mushrooms, and tomatoes onto 8 bamboo or metal skewers that fit in the air fryer. 4.Air fry at 200°C for 5 to 7 minutes, or until the beef is browned and reaches at least 64°C on a meat thermometer. 5.Serve immediately.

Mushroom and Green Bean Casserole

Prep time: 10 minutes | Cook time: 15 minutes | Serves 4

- 4 tablespoons unsalted butter
- 60 g diced brown onion
- 120 g chopped white mushrooms
- 120 ml double cream
- 30 g full fat soft white cheese
- 120 g chicken broth
- ¼ teaspoon xanthan gum
- 450 g fresh green beans, edges trimmed
- 14 g pork crackling, finely ground

1. In a medium skillet over medium heat, melt the butter 2.Sauté the onion and mushrooms until they become soft and fragrant, about 3 to 5 minutes 3.Add the double cream, soft white cheese, and broth to the pan 4.Whisk until smooth 5.Bring to a boil and then reduce to a simmer 6.Sprinkle the xanthan gum into the pan and remove from heat 7.Preheat the air fryer to 160°C 8.Chop the green beans into 2-inch pieces and place into a baking dish 9.Pour the sauce mixture over them and stir until coated 10.Top the dish with minced pork crackling 11.Put into the air fryer basket and bake for 15 minutes 12.Top will be golden and green beans fork-tender when fully cooked 13.Serve warm.

Pork Stuffing Meatballs

Prep time: 10 minutes | Cook time: 12 minutes | Makes 35 meatballs

- Oil, for spraying
- 680 g finely chopped pork
- 120 g breadcrumbs
- 120 ml milk
- 60 g finely chopped onion
- 1 large egg
- 1 tablespoon dried rosemary
- 1 tablespoon dried thyme
- 1 teaspoon salt
- 1 teaspoon ground black pepper
- 1 teaspoon finely chopped fresh parsley

1. Line the air fryer basket with parchment and spray lightly with oil. 2.In a large bowl, mix together the finely chopped pork, breadcrumbs, milk, onion, egg, rosemary, thyme, salt, black pepper, and parsley. 3.Roll about 2 tablespoons of the mixture into a ball. 4.Repeat with the rest of the mixture. You should have 30 to 35 meatballs. 5.Place the meatballs in the prepared basket in a single layer, leaving space between each one. You may need to work in batches, depending on the size of your air fryer. 6.Air fry at 200°C for 10 to 12 minutes, flipping after 5 minutes, or until golden brown and the internal temperature reaches 72°C.

Herb-Roasted Veggies

Prep time: 10 minutes | Cook time: 14 to 18 minutes | Serves 4

- 1 red pepper, sliced
- 1 (230 g) package sliced mushrooms
- 235 g runner beans, cut into 2-inch pieces

- 80 g diced red onion
- 3 garlic cloves, sliced
- 1 teaspoon olive oil
- ½ teaspoon dried basil
- ½ teaspoon dried tarragon

1. Preheat the air fryer to 180°C. 2.In a medium bowl, mix the red pepper, mushrooms, runner beans, red onion, and garlic. 3.Drizzle with the olive oil. Toss to coat. 4.Add the herbs and toss again. Place the vegetables in the air fryer basket. 5.Roast for 14 to 18 minutes, or until tender. 6.Serve immediately.

Cheesy Chilli Toast

Prep time: 5 minutes | Cook time: 5 minutes | Serves 1

- 2 tablespoons grated Parmesan cheese
- 2 tablespoons grated Mozzarella cheese
- 2 teaspoons salted butter, at room temperature
- 10 to 15 thin slices serrano chilli or jalapeño
- 2 slices sourdough bread
- ½ teaspoon black pepper

1. Preheat the air fryer to 160°C. 2.In a small bowl, stir together the Parmesan, Mozzarella, butter, and chillies. 3.Spread half the mixture onto one side of each slice of bread. 4.Sprinkle with the pepper. 5.Place the slices, cheese-side up, in the air fryer basket. 6.Bake for 5 minutes, or until the cheese has melted and started to brown slightly. 7.Serve immediately.

Scalloped Veggie Mix

Prep time: 10 minutes | Cook time: 15 minutes | Serves 4

- 1 Yukon Gold or other small white potato, thinly sliced
- 1 small sweet potato, peeled and thinly sliced
- 1 medium carrot, thinly sliced
- 60 g minced onion
- 3 garlic cloves, minced
- 180 ml 2 percent milk
- 2 tablespoons cornflour
- ½ teaspoon dried thyme

1. Preheat the air fryer to 190°C. 2.In a baking tray, layer the potato, sweet potato, carrot, onion, and garlic. 3.In a small bowl, whisk the milk, cornflour, and thyme until blended. 4.Pour the milk mixture evenly over the vegetables in the pan. Bake for 15 minutes. 5.Check the casserole—it should be golden brown on top, and the vegetables should be tender. 6.Serve immediately.

Simple Pea Delight

Prep time: 5 minutes | Cook time: 15 minutes | Serves 2 to 4

- 120 g flour
- 1 teaspoon baking powder
- 3 eggs
- 235 ml coconut milk
- 235 g soft white cheese
- 3 tablespoons pea protein
- 120 g chicken or turkey strips
- Pinch of sea salt
- 235 g Mozzarella cheese

1. Preheat the air fryer to 200°C. 2.In a large bowl, mix all ingredients together using a large wooden spoon. 3.Spoon equal amounts of the mixture into muffin cups and bake for 15 minutes. 4.Serve immediately.

Spinach and Carrot Balls

Prep time: 10 minutes | Cook time: 10 minutes | Serves 4

- 2 slices toasted bread
- 1 carrot, peeled and grated
- 1 package fresh spinach, blanched and chopped
- ½ onion, chopped
- 1 egg, beaten
- ½ teaspoon garlic powder
- 1 teaspoon minced garlic
- 1 teaspoon salt
- ½ teaspoon black pepper
- 1 tablespoon Engevita yeast flakes
- 1 tablespoon flour

1. Preheat the air fryer to 200°C. 2.In a food processor, pulse the toasted bread to form breadcrumbs. 3.Transfer into a shallow dish or bowl. In a bowl, mix together all the other ingredients. 4.Use your hands to shape the mixture into small-sized balls. 5.Roll the balls in the breadcrumbs, ensuring to cover them well. 6.Put in the air fryer basket and air fry for 10 minutes. 7.Serve immediately.

Sweet Maize and Carrot Fritters

Prep time: 10 minutes | Cook time: 8 to 11 minutes | Serves 4

- 1 medium-sized carrot, grated
- 1 brown onion, finely chopped
- 4 ounces (113 g) canned sweet maize kernels,

- drained
- 1 teaspoon sea salt flakes
- 1 tablespoon chopped fresh coriander
- 1 medium-sized egg, whisked
- 2 tablespoons plain milk
- 1 cup grated Parmesan cheese
- ¼ cup flour
- ⅓ teaspoon baking powder
- ⅓ teaspoon sugar
- Cooking spray

1. Preheat the air fryer to 350°F (177°C). 2. Place the grated carrot in a colander and press down to squeeze out any excess moisture. Dry it with a paper towel. 3. Combine the carrots with the remaining ingredients. 4. Mold 1 tablespoon of the mixture into a ball and press it down with your hand or a spoon to flatten it. Repeat until the rest of the mixture is used up. 5. Spritz the balls with cooking spray. 6. Arrange in the air fryer basket, taking care not to overlap any balls. Bake for 8 to 11 minutes, or until they're firm. 7. Serve warm.

Air Fried Courgette Sticks

Prep time: 5 minutes | Cook time: 20 minutes | Serves 4

- 1 medium courgette, cut into 48 sticks
- 30 g seasoned breadcrumbs
- 1 tablespoon melted margarine
- Cooking spray

1. Preheat the air fryer to 180°C. Spritz the air fryer basket with cooking spray and set aside. In 2 different shallow bowls, add the seasoned breadcrumbs and the margarine. One by one, dredge the courgette sticks into the margarine, then roll in the breadcrumbs to coat evenly. Arrange the crusted sticks on a plate. Place the courgette sticks in the prepared air fryer basket. Work in two batches to avoid overcrowding. Air fry for 10 minutes, or until golden brown and crispy. Shake the basket halfway through to cook evenly. When the cooking time is over, transfer the fries to a wire rack. Rest for 5 minutes and serve warm.

CHAPTER 3 Poultry and Meat

Butter and Bacon Chicken

Prep time: 10 minutes | Cook time: 65 minutes | Serves 6

1 (1.8 kg) whole chicken
- 2 tablespoons salted butter, softened
- 1 teaspoon dried thyme
- ½ teaspoon garlic powder
- 1 teaspoon salt
- ½ teaspoon ground black pepper
- 6 slices sugar-free bacon

1. Pat chicken dry with a paper towel, then rub with butter on all sides. Sprinkle thyme, garlic powder, salt, and pepper over chicken. 2. Place chicken into ungreased air fryer basket, breast side up. Lay strips of bacon over chicken and secure with toothpicks. 3. Adjust the temperature to 180°C and air fry for 65 minutes. Halfway through cooking, remove and set aside bacon and flip chicken over. Chicken will be done when the skin is golden and crispy and the internal temperature is at least 76°C. Serve warm with bacon.

Harissa-Rubbed Chicken

Prep time: 30 minutes | Cook time: 21 minutes | Serves 4

- Harissa:
- 120 ml olive oil
- 6 cloves garlic, minced
- 2 tablespoons smoked paprika
- 1 tablespoon ground coriander
- 1 tablespoon ground cumin
- 1 teaspoon ground caraway
- 1 teaspoon kosher salt
- ½ to 1 teaspoon cayenne pepper
- Chickens:
- 120 g yoghurt
- 2 small chickens, any giblets removed, split in half lengthwise

1. For the harissa: In a medium microwave-safe bowl, combine the oil, garlic, paprika, coriander, cumin, caraway, salt, and cayenne. Microwave on high for 1 minute, stirring halfway through the cooking time. (You tin also heat this on the stovetop until the oil is hot and bubbling. Or, if you must use your air fryer for everything, cook it in the air fryer at 180°C for 5 to 6 minutes, or until the paste is heated through.) 2. For the chicken: In a small bowl, combine 1 to 2 tablespoons harissa and the yoghurt. Whisk until well combined. Place the chicken halves in a resealable plastic bag and pour the marinade over. Seal the bag and massage until all of the pieces are thoroughly coated. Marinate at room temperature for 30 minutes or in the refrigerator for up to 24 hours. 3. Arrange the hen halves in a single layer in the air fryer basket. (If you have a smaller air fryer, you may have to cook this in two batches.) Set the air fryer to 200°C for 20 minutes. Use a meat thermometer to ensure the chickens have reached an internal temperature of 76°C.

Greek Chicken Souvlaki

Prep time: 30 minutes | Cook time: 15 minutes | Serves 3 to 4

- Chicken:
- Grated zest and juice of 1 lemon
- 2 tablespoons extra-virgin olive oil
- 1 tablespoon Greek souvlaki seasoning
- 450 g boneless, skinless chicken breast, cut into 2-inch chunks
- Vegetable oil spray
- For Serving:
- Warm pita bread or hot cooked rice
- Sliced ripe tomatoes
- Sliced cucumbers
- Thinly sliced red onion
- Kalamata olives
- Tzatziki

1. For the chicken: In a small bowl, combine the lemon zest, lemon juice, olive oil, and souvlaki seasoning. Place the chicken in a gallon-size resealable plastic bag. Pour the marinade over chicken. Seal bag and massage to coat. Place the bag in a large bowl and marinate for 30 minutes, or cover and refrigerate up to 24 hours, turning the bag occasionally. 2. Place the chicken a single layer in the air fryer basket. Set the air fryer to 180°C for 10 minutes, turning the chicken and spraying with a little

vegetable oil spray halfway through the cooking time. Increase the air fryer temperature to 200ºC for 5 minutes to allow the chicken to crisp and brown a little. 3. Transfer the chicken to a serving platter and serve with pita bread or rice, tomatoes, cucumbers, onion, olives and tzatziki.

Bacon-Wrapped Chicken Breasts Rolls

Prep time: 10 minutes | Cook time: 15 minutes | Serves 4

- 15 g chopped fresh chives
- 2 tablespoons lemon juice
- 1 teaspoon dried sage
- 1 teaspoon fresh rosemary leaves
- 15 g fresh parsley leaves
- 4 cloves garlic, peeled
- 1 teaspoon ground fennel
- 3 teaspoons sea salt
- ½ teaspoon red pepper flakes
- 4 (115 g) boneless, skinless chicken breasts, pounded to ¼ inch thick
- 8 slices bacon
- Sprigs of fresh rosemary, for garnish
- Cooking spray

1. Preheat the air fryer to 170ºC. Spritz the air fryer basket with cooking spray. 2. Put the chives, lemon juice, sage, rosemary, parsley, garlic, fennel, salt, and red pepper flakes in a food processor, then pulse to purée until smooth. 3. Unfold the chicken breasts on a clean work surface, then brush the top side of the chicken breasts with the sauce. 4. Roll the chicken breasts up from the shorter side, then wrap each chicken rolls with 2 bacon slices to cover. Secure with toothpicks. 5. Arrange the rolls in the preheated air fryer, then cook for 10 minutes. Flip the rolls halfway through. 6. Increase the heat to 200ºC and air fry for 5 more minutes or until the bacon is browned and crispy. 7. Transfer the rolls to a large plate. Discard the toothpicks and spread with rosemary sprigs before serving.

Coriander Lime Chicken Thighs

Prep time: 15 minutes | Cook time: 22 minutes | Serves 4

- 4 bone-in, skin-on chicken thighs
- 1 teaspoon baking powder
- ½ teaspoon garlic powder
- 2 teaspoons chilli powder
- 1 teaspoon cumin
- 2 medium limes
- 5 g chopped fresh coriander

1. Pat chicken thighs dry and sprinkle with baking powder. 2. In a small bowl, mix garlic powder, chilli powder, and cumin and sprinkle evenly over thighs, gently rubbing on and under chicken skin. 3. Cut one lime in half and squeeze juice over thighs. Place chicken into the air fryer basket. 4. Adjust the temperature to 190ºC and roast for 22 minutes. 5. Cut other lime into four wedges for serving and garnish cooked chicken with wedges and coriander.

Lemon-Basil Turkey Breasts

Prep time: 30 minutes | Cook time: 58 minutes | Serves 4

- 2 tablespoons olive oil
- 900 g turkey breasts, bone-in, skin-on
- Coarse sea salt and ground black pepper, to taste
- 1 teaspoon fresh basil leaves, chopped
- 2 tablespoons lemon zest, grated

1. Rub olive oil on all sides of the turkey breasts; sprinkle with salt, pepper, basil, and lemon zest. 2. Place the turkey breasts skin side up on the parchment-lined air fryer basket. 3. Cook in the preheated air fryer at 170ºC for 30 minutes. Now, turn them over and cook an additional 28 minutes. 4. Serve with lemon wedges, if desired. Bon appétit!

Blackened Chicken

Prep time: 10 minutes | Cook time: 20 minutes | Serves 4

- 1 large egg, beaten
- 215 g Blackened seasoning
- 2 whole boneless, skinless chicken breasts (about 450 g each), halved
- 1 to 2 tablespoons oil

1. Place the beaten egg in one shallow bowl and the Blackened seasoning in another shallow bowl. 2. One at a time, dip the chicken pieces in the beaten egg and the Blackened seasoning, coating thoroughly. 3. Preheat the air fryer to 180ºC. Line the air fryer basket with parchment paper. 4. Place the chicken pieces on the parchment and spritz with oil. 5. Cook for 10 minutes. Flip the chicken, spritz it with oil, and cook for 10 minutes more until the internal temperature reaches 76ºC and the chicken is no longer pink inside. Let sit for 5 minutes before serving.

Chicken and Gruyère Cordon Bleu

Prep time: 15 minutes | Cook time: 15 minutes | Serves 4

- 4 chicken breast filets
- 75 g chopped gammon
- 75 g grated Swiss cheese, or Gruyère cheese
- 15 g plain flour
- Pinch salt
- Freshly ground black pepper, to taste
- ½ teaspoon dried marjoram
- 1 egg
- 60 g panko bread crumbs
- Olive oil spray

1. Put the chicken breast filets on a work surface and gently press them with the palm of your hand to make them a bit thinner. Don't tear the meat. 2. In a small bowl, combine the gammon and cheese. Divide this mixture among the chicken filets. Wrap the chicken around the filling to enclose it, using toothpicks to hold the chicken together. 3. In a shallow bowl, stir together the flour, salt, pepper, and marjoram. 4. In another bowl, beat the egg. 5. Spread the panko on a plate. 6. Dip the chicken in the flour mixture, in the egg, and in the panko to coat thoroughly. Press the crumbs into the chicken so they stick well. 7. Insert the crisper plate into the basket and the basket into the unit. Preheat the unit by selecting BAKE, setting the temperature to 190ºC, and setting the time to 3 minutes. Select START/STOP to begin. 8. Once the unit is preheated, spray the crisper plate with olive oil. Place the chicken into the basket and spray it with olive oil. 9. Select BAKE, set the temperature to 190ºC, and set the time to 15 minutes. Select START/STOP to begin. 10. When the cooking is complete, the chicken should be cooked through and a food thermometer inserted into the chicken should register 76ºC. Carefully remove the toothpicks and serve.

Lemon-Dijon Boneless Chicken

Prep time: 30 minutes | Cook time: 13 to 16 minutes | Serves 6

- 115 g sugar-free mayonnaise
- 1 tablespoon Dijon mustard
- 1 tablespoon freshly squeezed lemon juice (optional)
- 1 tablespoon coconut aminos
- 1 teaspoon Italian seasoning
- 1 teaspoon sea salt
- ½ teaspoon freshly ground black pepper
- ¼ teaspoon cayenne pepper
- 680 g boneless, skinless chicken breasts or thighs

1. In a small bowl, combine the mayonnaise, mustard, lemon juice (if using), coconut aminos, Italian seasoning, salt, black pepper, and cayenne pepper. 2. Place the chicken in a shallow dish or large zip-top plastic bag. Add the marinade, making sure all the pieces are coated. Cover and refrigerate for at least 30 minutes or up to 4 hours. 3. Set the air fryer to 200ºC. Arrange the chicken in a single layer in the air fryer basket, working in batches if necessary. Air fry for 7 minutes. Flip the chicken and continue cooking for 6 to 9 minutes more, until an instant-read thermometer reads 70ºC.

Blackened Cajun Chicken Tenders

Prep time: 10 minutes | Cook time: 17 minutes | Serves 4

- 2 teaspoons paprika
- 1 teaspoon chilli powder
- ½ teaspoon garlic powder
- ½ teaspoon dried thyme
- ¼ teaspoon onion powder
- ⅛ teaspoon ground cayenne pepper
- 2 tablespoons coconut oil
- 450 g boneless, skinless chicken tenders
- 60 ml full-fat ranch dressing

1. In a small bowl, combine all seasonings. 2. Drizzle oil over chicken tenders and then generously coat each tender in the spice mixture. Place tenders into the air fryer basket. 3. Adjust the temperature to (190ºC and air fry for 17 minutes. 4. Tenders will be 76ºC internally when fully cooked. Serve with ranch dressing for dipping.

Turkish Chicken Kebabs

Prep time: 30 minutes | Cook time: 15 minutes | Serves 4

- 70 g plain Greek yoghurt
- 1 tablespoon minced garlic
- 1 tablespoon tomato paste
- 1 tablespoon fresh lemon juice
- 1 tablespoon vegetable oil
- 1 teaspoon kosher salt
- 1 teaspoon ground cumin
- 1 teaspoon sweet Hungarian paprika

- ½ teaspoon ground cinnamon
- ½ teaspoon black pepper
- ½ teaspoon cayenne pepper
- 450 g boneless, skinless chicken thighs, quartered crosswise

1. In a large bowl, combine the yoghurt, garlic, tomato paste, lemon juice, vegetable oil, salt, cumin, paprika, cinnamon, black pepper, and cayenne. Stir until the spices are blended into the yoghurt. 2. Add the chicken to the bowl and toss until well coated. Marinate at room temperature for 30 minutes, or cover and refrigerate for up to 24 hours. 3. Arrange the chicken in a single layer in the air fryer basket. Set the air fryer to (190°C for 10 minutes. Turn the chicken and cook for 5 minutes more. Use a meat thermometer to ensure the chicken has reached an internal temperature of 76°C.

Mediterranean Stuffed Chicken Breasts

Prep time: 5 minutes | Cook time: 20 to 25 minutes | Serves 4

- 4 small boneless, skinless chicken breast halves (about 680 g)
- Salt and freshly ground black pepper, to taste
- 115 g goat cheese
- 6 pitted Kalamata olives, coarsely chopped
- Zest of ½ lemon
- 1 teaspoon minced fresh rosemary or ½ teaspoon ground dried rosemary
- 25 g ground almonds
- 60 ml balsamic vinegar
- 6 tablespoons unsalted butter

1. Preheat the air fryer to 180°C. 2. With a boning knife, cut a wide pocket into the thickest part of each chicken breast half, taking care not to cut all the way through. Season the chicken evenly on both sides with salt and freshly ground black pepper. 3. In a small bowl, mix the cheese, olives, lemon zest, and rosemary. Stuff the pockets with the cheese mixture and secure with toothpicks. 4. Place the ground almonds in a shallow bowl and dredge the chicken, shaking off the excess. Coat lightly with olive oil spray. 5. Working in batches if necessary, arrange the chicken breasts in a single layer in the air fryer basket. Pausing halfway through the cooking time to flip the chicken, air fry for 20 to 25 minutes, until a thermometer inserted into the thickest part registers 76°C. 6. While the chicken is baking, prepare the sauce. In a small pan over medium heat, simmer the balsamic vinegar until thick and syrupy, about 5 minutes. Set aside until the chicken is done. When ready to serve, warm the sauce over medium heat and whisk in the butter, 1 tablespoon at a time, until melted and smooth. Season to taste with salt and pepper. 7. Serve the chicken breasts with the sauce drizzled on top.

Chicken Strips with Satay Sauce

Prep time: 15 minutes | Cook time: 10 minutes | Serves 4

- 4 (170 g) boneless, skinless chicken breasts, sliced into 16 (1-inch) strips
- 1 teaspoon fine sea salt
- 1 teaspoon paprika
- Sauce:
- 60 g creamy almond butter (or sunflower seed butter for nut-free)
- 2 tablespoons chicken broth
- 1½ tablespoons coconut vinegar or unseasoned rice vinegar
- 1 clove garlic, minced
- 1 teaspoon peeled and minced fresh ginger
- ½ teaspoon hot sauce
- ⅛ teaspoon stevia glycerite, or 2 to 3 drops liquid stevia
- For Garnish/Serving (Optional):
- 15 g chopped coriander leaves
- Red pepper flakes
- Sea salt flakes
- Thinly sliced red, orange, and yellow peppers
- Special Equipment:
- 16 wooden or bamboo skewers, soaked in water for 15 minutes

1. Spray the air fryer basket with avocado oil. Preheat the air fryer to 200°C. 2. Thread the chicken strips onto the skewers. Season on all sides with the salt and paprika. Place the chicken skewers in the air fryer basket and air fry for 5 minutes, flip, and cook for another 5 minutes, until the chicken is cooked through and the internal temperature reaches 76°C. 3. While the chicken skewers cook, make the sauce: In a medium-sized bowl, stir together all the sauce ingredients until well combined. Taste and adjust the sweetness and heat to your liking. 4. Garnish the chicken with coriander, red pepper flakes, and salt flakes, if desired, and serve with sliced peppers, if desired.

Serve the sauce on the side. 5. Store leftovers in an airtight container in the fridge for up to 4 days or in the freezer for up to a month. Reheat in a preheated 180ºC air fryer for 3 minutes per side, or until heated through.

Ethiopian Chicken with Cauliflower

Prep time: 15 minutes | Cook time: 28 minutes | Serves 6

- 2 handful fresh Italian parsley, roughly chopped
- 20 g fresh chopped chives
- 2 sprigs thyme
- 6 chicken drumsticks
- 1½ small-sized head cauliflower, broken into large-sized florets
- 2 teaspoons mustard powder
- ⅓ teaspoon porcini powder
- 1½ teaspoons berbere spice
- ⅓ teaspoon sweet paprika
- ½ teaspoon shallot powder
- 1 teaspoon granulated garlic
- 1 teaspoon freshly cracked pink peppercorns
- ½ teaspoon sea salt

1. Simply combine all items for the berbere spice rub mix. After that, coat the chicken drumsticks with this rub mix on all sides. Transfer them to the baking dish. 2. Now, lower the cauliflower onto the chicken drumsticks. Add thyme, chives and Italian parsley and spritz everything with a pan spray. Transfer the baking dish to the preheated air fryer. 3. Next step, set the timer for 28 minutes; roast at 180ºC, turning occasionally. Bon appétit!

Bruschetta Chicken

Prep time: 10 minutes | Cook time: 20 minutes | Serves 4

- Bruschetta Stuffing:
- 1 tomato, diced
- 3 tablespoons balsamic vinegar
- 1 teaspoon Italian seasoning
- 2 tablespoons chopped fresh basil
- 3 garlic cloves, minced
- 2 tablespoons extra-virgin olive oil
- Chicken:
- 4 (115 g) boneless, skinless chicken breasts, cut 4 slits each
- 1 teaspoon Italian seasoning
- Chicken seasoning or rub, to taste
- Cooking spray

1. Preheat the air fryer to 190º. Spritz the air fryer basket with cooking spray. 2. Combine the ingredients for the bruschetta stuffing in a bowl. Stir to mix well. Set aside. 3. Rub the chicken breasts with Italian seasoning and chicken seasoning on a clean work surface. 4. Arrange the chicken breasts, slits side up, in a single layer in the air fryer basket and spritz with cooking spray. You may need to work in batches to avoid overcrowding. 5. Air fry for 7 minutes, then open the air fryer and fill the slits in the chicken with the bruschetta stuffing. Cook for another 3 minutes or until the chicken is well browned. 6. Serve immediately.

Golden Chicken Cutlets

Prep time: 15 minutes | Cook time: 15 minutes | Serves 4

- 2 tablespoons panko breadcrumbs
- 20 g grated Parmesan cheese
- ⅛ tablespoon paprika
- ½ tablespoon garlic powder
- 2 large eggs
- 4 chicken cutlets
- 1 tablespoon parsley
- Salt and ground black pepper, to taste
- Cooking spray

1. Preheat air fryer to 200ºC. Spritz the air fryer basket with cooking spray. 2. Combine the breadcrumbs, Parmesan, paprika, garlic powder, salt, and ground black pepper in a large bowl. Stir to mix well. Beat the eggs in a separate bowl. 3. Dredge the chicken cutlets in the beaten eggs, then roll over the breadcrumbs mixture to coat well. Shake the excess off. 4. Transfer the chicken cutlets in the preheated air fryer and spritz with cooking spray. 5. Air fry for 15 minutes or until crispy and golden brown. Flip the cutlets halfway through. 6. Serve with parsley on top.

Chipotle Drumsticks

Prep time: 15 minutes | Cook time: 20 minutes | Serves 4

- 1 tablespoon tomato paste
- ½ teaspoon chipotle powder
- ¼ teaspoon apple cider vinegar
- ¼ teaspoon garlic powder
- 8 chicken drumsticks

- ½ teaspoon salt
- ⅛ teaspoon ground black pepper

1. In a small bowl, combine tomato paste, chipotle powder, vinegar, and garlic powder. 2. Sprinkle drumsticks with salt and pepper, then place into a large bowl and pour in tomato paste mixture. Toss or stir to evenly coat all drumsticks in mixture. 3. Place drumsticks into ungreased air fryer basket. Adjust the temperature to 200°C and air fry for 25 minutes, turning drumsticks halfway through cooking. Drumsticks will be dark red with an internal temperature of at least 76°C when done. Serve warm.

Almond-Crusted Chicken

Prep time: 15 minutes | Cook time: 25 minutes | Serves 4

- 20 g slivered almonds
- 2 (170 g) boneless, skinless chicken breasts
- 2 tablespoons full-fat mayonnaise
- 1 tablespoon Dijon mustard

1. Pulse the almonds in a food processor or chop until finely chopped. Place almonds evenly on a plate and set aside. 2. Completely slice each chicken breast in half lengthwise. 3. Mix the mayonnaise and mustard in a small bowl and then coat chicken with the mixture. 4. Lay each piece of chicken in the chopped almonds to fully coat. Carefully move the pieces into the air fryer basket. 5. Adjust the temperature to 180°C and air fry for 25 minutes. 6. Chicken will be done when it has reached an internal temperature of 76°C or more. Serve warm.

Sweet Chili Spiced Chicken

Prep time: 10 minutes | Cook time: 43 minutes | Serves 4

- Spice Rub:
- 2 tablespoons brown sugar
- 2 tablespoons paprika
- 1 teaspoon dry mustard powder
- 1 teaspoon chilli powder
- 2 tablespoons coarse sea salt or kosher salt
- 2 teaspoons coarsely ground black pepper
- 1 tablespoon vegetable oil

1 (1.6 kg) chicken, cut into 8 pieces

1. Prepare the spice rub by combining the brown sugar, paprika, mustard powder, chilli powder, salt and pepper. Rub the oil all over the chicken pieces and then rub the spice mix onto the chicken, covering completely. This is done very easily in a zipper sealable bag. You tin do this ahead of time and let the chicken marinate in the refrigerator, or just proceed with cooking right away. 2. Preheat the air fryer to 190°C. 3. Air fry the chicken in two batches. Place the two chicken thighs and two drumsticks into the air fryer basket. Air fry at 190°C for 10 minutes. Then, gently turn the chicken pieces over and air fry for another 10 minutes. Remove the chicken pieces and let them rest on a plate while you cook the chicken breasts. Air fry the chicken breasts, skin side down for 8 minutes. Turn the chicken breasts over and air fry for another 12 minutes. 4. Lower the temperature of the air fryer to 170°C. Place the first batch of chicken on top of the second batch already in the basket and air fry for a final 3 minutes. 5. Let the chicken rest for 5 minutes and serve warm with some mashed potatoes and a green salad or vegetables.

Bacon-Wrapped Stuffed Chicken Breasts

Prep time: 15 minutes | Cook time: 30 minutes | Serves 4

- 80 g chopped frozen spinach, thawed and squeezed dry
- 55 g cream cheese, softened
- 20 g grated Parmesan cheese
- 1 jalapeño, seeded and chopped
- ½ teaspoon kosher salt
- 1 teaspoon black pepper
- 2 large boneless, skinless chicken breasts, butterflied and pounded to ½-inch thickness
- 4 teaspoons salt-free Cajun seasoning
- 6 slices bacon

1. In a small bowl, combine the spinach, cream cheese, Parmesan cheese, jalapeño, salt, and pepper. Stir until well combined. 2. Place the butterflied chicken breasts on a flat surface. Spread the cream cheese mixture evenly across each piece of chicken. Starting with the narrow end, roll up each chicken breast, ensuring the filling stays inside. Season chicken with the Cajun seasoning, patting it in to ensure it sticks to the meat. 3. Wrap each breast in 3 slices of bacon. Place in the air fryer basket. Set the air fryer to 180°C for 30 minutes. Use a meat thermometer to ensure the chicken has reached an internal temperature of 76°C. 4. Let the chicken stand 5 minutes before slicing each rolled-up breast in half to serve.

Barbecue Chicken Bites

Prep time: 5 minutes | Cook time: 19 minutes | Serves 4

- Oil, for spraying
- 2 (170 g) boneless, skinless chicken breasts, cut into bite-size pieces
- 30 g plain flour
- 1 tablespoon granulated garlic
- 2 teaspoons seasoned salt
- 280 g barbecue sauce

1. Line the air fryer basket with parchment and spray lightly with oil. 2. Place the chicken, flour, garlic, and seasoned salt in a zip-top plastic bag, seal, and shake well until evenly coated. 3. Place the chicken in an even layer in the prepared basket and spray liberally with oil. You may need to work in batches, depending on the size of your air fryer. 4. Roast at 200°C for 8 minutes, flip, spray with more oil, and cook for another 8 minutes, or until the internal temperature reaches 76°C and the juices run clear. 5. Transfer the chicken to a large bowl and toss with the barbecue sauce. 6. Line the air fryer basket with fresh parchment, return the chicken to the basket, and cook for another 3 minutes.

Garlic Soy Chicken Thighs

Prep time: 10 minutes | Cook time: 30 minutes | Serves 1 to 2

- 2 tablespoons chicken stock
- 2 tablespoons reduced-sodium soy sauce
- 1½ tablespoons sugar
- 4 garlic cloves, smashed and peeled
- 2 large spring onions, cut into 2- to 3-inch batons, plus more, thinly sliced, for garnish
- 2 bone-in, skin-on chicken thighs (198 to 225 g each)

1. Preheat the air fryer to 190°C. 2. In a metal cake pan, combine the chicken stock, soy sauce, and sugar and stir until the sugar dissolves. Add the garlic cloves, spring onions, and chicken thighs, turning the thighs to coat them in the marinade, then resting them skin-side up. Place the pan in the air fryer and bake, flipping the thighs every 5 minutes after the first 10 minutes, until the chicken is cooked through and the marinade is reduced to a sticky glaze over the chicken, about 30 minutes. 3. Remove the pan from the air fryer and serve the chicken thighs warm, with any remaining glaze spooned over top and sprinkled with more sliced spring onions.

Italian Crispy Chicken

Prep time: 10 minutes | Cook time: 20 minutes | Serves 4

- 2 (115 g) boneless, skinless chicken breasts
- 2 egg whites, beaten
- 60 g Italian bread crumbs
- 45 g grated Parmesan cheese
- 2 teaspoons Italian seasoning
- Salt and freshly ground black pepper, to taste
- Cooking oil spray
- 180 g marinara sauce
- 110 g shredded Mozzarella cheese

1. With your knife blade parallel to the cutting board, cut the chicken breasts in half horizontally to create 4 thin cutlets. On a solid surface, pound the cutlets to flatten them. You tin use your hands, a rolling pin, a kitchen mallet, or a meat hammer. 2. Pour the egg whites into a bowl large enough to dip the chicken. 3. In another bowl large enough to dip a chicken cutlet in, stir together the bread crumbs, Parmesan cheese, and Italian seasoning, and season with salt and pepper. 4. Dip each cutlet into the egg whites and into the breadcrumb mixture to coat. 5. Insert the crisper plate into the basket and the basket into the unit. Preheat the unit by selecting AIR FRY, setting the temperature to 190°C, and setting the time to 3 minutes. Select START/STOP to begin. 6. Once the unit is preheated, spray the crisper plate with cooking oil. Working in batches, place 2 chicken cutlets into the basket. Spray the top of the chicken with cooking oil. 7. Select AIR FRY, set the temperature to 190°C, and set the time to 7 minutes. Select START/STOP to begin. 8. When the cooking is complete, repeat steps 6 and 7 with the remaining cutlets. 9. Top the chicken cutlets with the marinara sauce and shredded Mozzarella cheese. If the chicken will fit into the basket without stacking, you tin prepare all 4 at once. Otherwise, do this 2 cutlets at a time. 10. Select AIR FRY, set the temperature to 190°C, and set the time to 3 minutes. Select START/STOP to begin. 11. The cooking is complete when the cheese is melted and the chicken reaches an internal temperature of 76°C. Cool for 5 minutes before serving.

Chicken Thighs with Coriander

Prep time: 15 minutes | Cook time: 25 minutes | Serves 4

- 1 tablespoon olive oil

- Juice of ½ lime
- 1 tablespoon coconut aminos
- 1½ teaspoons Montreal chicken seasoning
- 8 bone-in chicken thighs, skin on
- 2 tablespoons chopped fresh coriander

1. In a gallon-size resealable bag, combine the olive oil, lime juice, coconut aminos, and chicken seasoning. Add the chicken thighs, seal the bag, and massage the bag to ensure the chicken is thoroughly coated. Refrigerate for at least 2 hours, preferably overnight. 2. Preheat the air fryer to 200°C. 3. Remove the chicken from the marinade (discard the marinade) and arrange in a single layer in the air fryer basket. Pausing halfway through the cooking time to flip the chicken, air fry for 20 to 25 minutes, until a thermometer inserted into the thickest part registers 76°C. 4. Transfer the chicken to a serving platter and top with the coriander before serving.

Chicken Hand Pies

Prep time: 30 minutes | Cook time: 10 minutes per batch | Makes 8 pies

- 180 ml chicken broth
- 130 g frozen mixed peas and carrots
- 140 g cooked chicken, chopped
- 1 tablespoon cornflour
- 1 tablespoon milk
- Salt and pepper, to taste
- 1 (8-count) tin organic flaky biscuits
- Oil for misting or cooking spray

1. In a medium saucepan, bring chicken broth to a boil. Stir in the frozen peas and carrots and cook for 5 minutes over medium heat. Stir in chicken. 2. Mix the cornflour into the milk until it dissolves. Stir it into the simmering chicken broth mixture and cook just until thickened. 3. Remove from heat, add salt and pepper to taste, and let cool slightly. 4. Lay biscuits out on wax paper. Peel each biscuit apart in the middle to make 2 rounds so you have 16 rounds total. Using your hands or a rolling pin, flatten each biscuit round slightly to make it larger and thinner. 5. Divide chicken filling among 8 of the biscuit rounds. Place remaining biscuit rounds on top and press edges all around. Use the tines of a fork to crimp biscuit edges and make sure they are sealed well. 6. Spray both sides lightly with oil or cooking spray. 7. Cook in a single layer, 4 at a time, at 170°C for 10 minutes or until biscuit dough is cooked through and golden brown.

CHAPTER 4 Beef, Pork, and Lamb

Beefy Poppers

Prep time: 15 minutes | Cook time: 15 minutes | Makes 8 poppers

- 8 medium red chillis, stemmed, halved, and seeded
- 1 (230 g) package cream cheese (or cream cheese style spread for dairy-free), softened
- 900 g beef mince (85% lean)
- 1 teaspoon fine sea salt
- ½ teaspoon ground black pepper
- 8 slices thin-cut bacon
- Fresh coriander leaves, for garnish

1. Spray the air fryer basket with avocado oil. Preheat the air fryer to 200°C. 2. Stuff each jalapeño half with a few tablespoons of cream cheese. Place the halves back together again to form 8 jalapeños. 3. Season the beef mince with the salt and pepper and mix with your hands to incorporate. Flatten about 110 g of beef in the palm of your hand and place a stuffed jalapeño in the center. Fold the beef around the jalapeño, forming an egg shape. Wrap the beef-covered jalapeño with rasher and secure it with a toothpick. 4. Place the jalapeños in the air fryer basket, leaving space between them (if you're using a smaller air fryer, work in batches if necessary), and air fry for 15 minutes, or until the beef is cooked through and the bacon is crispy. Garnish with coriander before serving. 5. Store leftovers in an airtight container in the fridge for 3 days or in the freezer for up to a month. Reheat in a preheated 180°C air fryer for 4 minutes, or until heated through and the bacon is crispy.

Banger and Cauliflower Arancini

Prep time: 30 minutes | Cook time: 28 to 32 minutes | Serves 6

- Avocado oil spray
- 170 g Italian-seasoned banger, casings removed
- 60 g diced onion
- 1 teaspoon minced garlic
- 1 teaspoon dried thyme
- Sea salt and freshly ground black pepper, to taste
- 120 g cauliflower rice
- 85 g cream cheese
- 110 g Cheddar cheese, shredded
- 1 large egg
- 60 g finely ground blanched almond flour
- 60 g finely grated Parmesan cheese
- Keto-friendly marinara sauce, for serving

1. Spray a large frying pan with oil and place it over medium-high heat. Once the frying pan is hot, put the banger in the frying pan and cook for 7 minutes, breaking up the meat with the back of a spoon. 2. Reduce the heat to medium and add the onion. Cook for 5 minutes, then add the garlic, thyme, and salt and pepper to taste. Cook for 1 minute more. 3. Add the cauliflower rice and cream cheese to the frying pan. Cook for 7 minutes, stirring frequently, until the cream cheese melts and the cauliflower is tender. 4. Remove the frying pan from the heat and stir in the Cheddar cheese. Using a biscuit scoop, form the mixture into 1½-inch balls. Place the balls on a parchment paper-lined baking sheet. Freeze for 30 minutes. 5. Place the egg in a shallow bowl and beat it with a fork. In a separate bowl, stir together the almond flour and Parmesan cheese. 6. Dip the cauliflower balls into the egg, then coat them with the almond flour mixture, gently pressing the mixture to the balls to adhere. 7. Set the air fryer to 200°C. Spray the cauliflower rice balls with oil, and arrange them in a single layer in the air fryer basket, working in batches if necessary. Air fry for 5 minutes. Flip the rice balls and spray them with more oil. Air fry for 3 to 7 minutes longer, until the balls are golden brown. 8. Serve warm with marinara sauce.

Five-Spice Pork Belly

Prep time: 10 minutes | Cook time: 17 minutes | Serves 4

- 450 g unsalted pork belly
- 2 teaspoons Chinese five-spice powder
- Sauce:
- 1 tablespoon coconut oil
- 1 (1-inch) piece fresh ginger, peeled and grated
- 2 cloves garlic, minced
- 120 ml beef or chicken stock
- ¼ to 120 ml liquid or powdered sweetener
- 3 tablespoons wheat-free tamari

- 1 spring onion, sliced, plus more for garnish

1. Spray the air fryer basket with avocado oil. Preheat the air fryer to 200°C. 2. Cut the pork belly into ½-inch-thick slices and season well on all sides with the five-spice powder. Place the slices in a single layer in the air fryer basket (if you're using a smaller air fryer, work in batches if necessary) and cook for 8 minutes, or until cooked to your liking, flipping halfway through. 3. While the pork belly cooks, make the sauce: Heat the coconut oil in a small saucepan over medium heat. Add the ginger and garlic and sauté for 1 minute, or until fragrant. Add the stock, sweetener, and tamari and simmer for 10 to 15 minutes, until thickened. Add the spring onion and cook for another minute, until the spring onion is softened. Taste and adjust the seasoning to your liking. 4. Transfer the pork belly to a large bowl. Pour the sauce over the pork belly and coat well. Place the pork belly slices on a serving platter and garnish with sliced spring onions. 5. Best served fresh. Store leftovers in an airtight container in the fridge for up to 4 days. Reheat in a preheated 200°C air fryer for 3 minutes, or until heated through.

Herb-Crusted Lamb Chops

Prep time: 10 minutes | Cook time: 5 minutes | Serves 2

- 1 large egg
- 2 cloves garlic, minced
- 60 g finely crushed pork scratchings
- 60 g pre-grated Parmesan cheese
- 1 tablespoon chopped fresh oregano leaves
- 1 tablespoon chopped fresh rosemary leaves
- 1 teaspoon chopped fresh thyme leaves
- ½ teaspoon ground black pepper
- 4 (1-inch-thick) lamb chops
- For Garnish/Serving (Optional):
- Sprigs of fresh oregano
- Sprigs of fresh rosemary
- Sprigs of fresh thyme
- Lavender flowers
- Lemon slices

1. Spray the air fryer basket with avocado oil. Preheat the air fryer to 200°C. 2. Beat the egg in a shallow bowl, add the garlic, and stir well to combine. In another shallow bowl, mix together the crushed pork scratchings, Parmesan, herbs, and pepper. 3. One at a time, dip the lamb chops into the egg mixture, shake off the excess egg, and then dredge them in the Parmesan mixture. Use your hands to coat the chops well in the Parmesan mixture and form a nice crust on all sides; if necessary, dip the chops again in both the egg and the Parmesan mixture. 4. Place the lamb chops in the air fryer basket, leaving space between them, and air fry for 5 minutes, or until the internal temperature reaches 64°C for medium doneness. Allow to rest for 10 minutes before serving. 5. Garnish with sprigs of oregano, rosemary, and thyme, and lavender flowers, if desired. Serve with lemon slices, if desired. 6. Best served fresh. Store leftovers in an airtight container in the fridge for up to 4 days. Serve chilled over a salad, or reheat in a 180°C air fryer for 3 minutes, or until heated through.

Sweet and Spicy Country-Style Ribs

Prep time: 10 minutes | Cook time: 25 minutes | Serves 4

- 2 tablespoons brown sugar
- 2 tablespoons smoked paprika
- 1 teaspoon garlic powder
- 1 teaspoon onion granules
- 1 teaspoon mustard powder
- 1 teaspoon ground cumin
- 1 teaspoon coarse or flaky salt
- 1 teaspoon black pepper
- ¼ to ½ teaspoon cayenne pepper
- 680 g boneless pork steaks
- 235 ml barbecue sauce

1. In a small bowl, stir together the brown sugar, paprika, garlic powder, onion granules, mustard powder, cumin, salt, black pepper, and cayenne. Mix until well combined. 2. Pat the ribs dry with a paper towel. Generously sprinkle the rub evenly over both sides of the ribs and rub in with your fingers. 3. Place the ribs in the air fryer basket. Set the air fryer to 180°C for 15 minutes. Turn the ribs and brush with 120 ml of the barbecue sauce. Cook for an additional 10 minutes. Use a meat thermometer to ensure the pork has reached an internal temperature of 64°C. 4. Serve with remaining barbecue sauce.

Beef Burger

Prep time: 20 minutes | Cook time: 12 minutes | Serves 4

- 570 g lean beef mince
- 1 tablespoon soy sauce or tamari
- 1 teaspoon Dijon mustard

- ½ teaspoon smoked paprika
- 1 teaspoon shallot powder
- 1 clove garlic, minced
- ½ teaspoon cumin powder
- 60 g spring onions, minced
- ⅓ teaspoon sea salt flakes
- ⅓ teaspoon freshly cracked mixed peppercorns
- 1 teaspoon celery salt
- 1 teaspoon dried parsley

1. Mix all of the above ingredients in a bowl; knead until everything is well incorporated. 2. Shape the mixture into four patties. Next, make a shallow dip in the center of each patty to prevent them puffing up during air frying. 3. Spritz the patties on all sides using nonstick cooking spray. Cook approximately 12 minutes at 180°C. 4. Check for doneness, an instant-read thermometer should read 72°C. Bon appétit!

Onion Pork Kebabs

Prep time: 22 minutes | Cook time: 18 minutes | Serves 3

- 2 tablespoons tomato purée
- ½ fresh green chilli, minced
- ⅓ teaspoon paprika
- 450 g pork mince
- 120 g spring onions, finely chopped
- 3 cloves garlic, peeled and finely minced
- 1 teaspoon ground black pepper, or more to taste
- 1 teaspoon salt, or more to taste

1. Thoroughly combine all ingredients in a mixing dish. Then form your mixture into banger shapes. 2. Cook for 18 minutes at 180°C. Mound salad on a serving platter, top with air-fried kebabs and serve warm. Bon appétit!

Bacon and Cheese Stuffed Pork Chops

Prep time: 10 minutes | Cook time: 12 minutes | Serves 4

- 15 g plain pork scratchings, finely crushed
- 120 g shredded sharp Cheddar cheese
- 4 slices cooked bacon, crumbled
- 4 (110 g) boneless pork chops
- ½ teaspoon salt
- ¼ teaspoon ground black pepper

1. In a small bowl, mix pork scratchings, Cheddar, and bacon. 2. Make a 3-inch slit in the side of each pork chop and stuff with ¼ pork rind mixture. Sprinkle each side of pork chops with salt and pepper. 3. Place pork chops into ungreased air fryer basket, stuffed side up. Adjust the temperature to 200°C and air fry for 12 minutes. Pork chops will be browned and have an internal temperature of at least 64°C when done. Serve warm.

Lamb Burger with Feta and Olives

Prep time: 10 minutes | Cook time: 20 minutes | Serves 3 to 4

- 2 teaspoons olive oil
- ⅓ onion, finely chopped
- 1 clove garlic, minced
- 450 g lamb mince
- 2 tablespoons fresh parsley, finely chopped
- 1½ teaspoons fresh oregano, finely chopped
- 120 g black olives, finely chopped
- 80 g crumbled feta cheese
- ½ teaspoon salt
- Freshly ground black pepper, to taste
- 4 thick pitta breads

1. Preheat a medium frying pan over medium-high heat on the stovetop. Add the olive oil and cook the onion until tender, but not browned, about 4 to 5 minutes. Add the garlic and cook for another minute. Transfer the onion and garlic to a mixing bowl and add the lamb mince, parsley, oregano, olives, feta cheese, salt and pepper. Gently mix the ingredients together. 2. Divide the mixture into 3 or 4 equal portions and then form the hamburgers, being careful not to over-handle the meat. One good way to do this is to throw the meat back and forth between your hands like a baseball, packing the meat each time you catch it. Flatten the balls into patties, making an indentation in the center of each patty. Flatten the sides of the patties as well to make it easier to fit them into the air fryer basket. 3. Preheat the air fryer to 190°C. 4. If you don't have room for all four burgers, air fry two or three burgers at a time for 8 minutes at 190°C. Flip the burgers over and air fry for another 8 minutes. If you cooked your burgers in batches, return the first batch of burgers to the air fryer for the last two minutes of cooking to re-heat. This should give you a medium-well burger. If you'd prefer a medium-rare burger, shorten the cooking time to about 13 minutes. Remove the burgers to a resting plate and let the burgers rest for a few minutes before dressing and serving. 5. While the burgers are resting, toast the pitta breads in the air fryer for 2 minutes. Tuck the burgers into the toasted pitta breads, or wrap the pittas around the burgers and serve with a

tzatziki sauce or some mayonnaise.

Spice-Rubbed Pork Loin

Prep time: 5 minutes | Cook time: 20 minutes | Serves 6

- 1 teaspoon paprika
- ½ teaspoon ground cumin
- ½ teaspoon chilli powder
- ½ teaspoon garlic powder
- 2 tablespoons coconut oil
- 1 (680 g) boneless pork loin
- ½ teaspoon salt
- ¼ teaspoon ground black pepper

1. In a small bowl, mix paprika, cumin, chilli powder, and garlic powder. 2. Drizzle coconut oil over pork. Sprinkle pork loin with salt and pepper, then rub spice mixture evenly on all sides. 3. Place pork loin into ungreased air fryer basket. Adjust the temperature to 204°C and air fry for 20 minutes, turning pork halfway through cooking. Pork loin will be browned and have an internal temperature of at least 64°C when done. Serve warm.

Blackened Steak Nuggets

Prep time: 10 minutes | Cook time: 7 minutes | Serves 2

- 450 g rib eye steak, cut into 1-inch cubes
- 2 tablespoons salted melted butter
- ½ teaspoon paprika
- ½ teaspoon salt
- ¼ teaspoon garlic powder
- ¼ teaspoon onion granules
- ¼ teaspoon ground black pepper
- ⅛ teaspoon cayenne pepper

1. Place steak into a large bowl and pour in butter. Toss to coat. Sprinkle with remaining ingredients. 2. Place bites into ungreased air fryer basket. Adjust the temperature to 200°C and air fry for 7 minutes, shaking the basket three times during cooking. Steak will be crispy on the outside and browned when done and internal temperature is at least 64°C for medium and 82°C for well-done. Serve warm.

Kheema Burgers

Prep time: 15 minutes | Cook time: 12 minutes | Serves 4

- Burgers:
- 450 g 85% lean beef mince or lamb mince
- 2 large eggs, lightly beaten
- 1 medium brown onion, diced
- 60 g chopped fresh coriander
- 1 tablespoon minced fresh ginger
- 3 cloves garlic, minced
- 2 teaspoons garam masala
- 1 teaspoon ground turmeric
- ½ teaspoon ground cinnamon
- ⅛ teaspoon ground cardamom
- 1 teaspoon coarse or flaky salt
- 1 teaspoon cayenne pepper
- Raita Sauce:
- 235 g grated cucumber
- 120 ml sour cream
- ¼ teaspoon coarse or flaky salt
- ¼ teaspoon black pepper
- For Serving:
- 4 lettuce leaves, hamburger buns, or naan breads

1. For the burgers: In a large bowl, combine the beef mince, eggs, onion, coriander, ginger, garlic, garam masala, turmeric, cinnamon, cardamom, salt, and cayenne. Gently mix until ingredients are thoroughly combined. 2. Divide the meat into four portions and form into round patties. Make a slight depression in the middle of each patty with your thumb to prevent them from puffing up into a dome shape while cooking. 3. Place the patties in the air fryer basket. Set the air fryer to 180°C for 12 minutes. Use a meat thermometer to ensure the burgers have reached an internal temperature of 72°C (for medium). 4. Meanwhile, for the sauce: In a small bowl, combine the cucumber, sour cream, salt, and pepper. 5. To serve: Place the burgers on the lettuce, buns, or naan and top with the sauce.

Beef Mince Taco Rolls

Prep time: 20 minutes | Cook time: 10 minutes | Serves 4

- 230 g 80/20 beef mince
- 80 ml water
- 1 tablespoon chilli powder
- 2 teaspoons cumin
- ½ teaspoon garlic powder
- ¼ teaspoon dried oregano
- 60 g tinned diced tomatoes
- 2 tablespoons chopped coriander

- 355 g shredded Mozzarella cheese
- 60 g blanched finely ground almond flour
- 60 g full-fat cream cheese
- 1 large egg

1. In a medium frying pan over medium heat, brown the beef mince about 7 to 10 minutes. When meat is fully cooked, drain. 2. Add water to frying pan and stir in chilli powder, cumin, garlic powder, oregano, and tomatoes. Add coriander. Bring to a boil, then reduce heat to simmer for 3 minutes. 3. In a large microwave-safe bowl, place Mozzarella, almond flour, cream cheese, and egg. Microwave for 1 minute. Stir the mixture quickly until smooth ball of dough forms. 4. Cut a piece of parchment for your work surface. Press the dough into a large rectangle on the parchment, wetting your hands to prevent the dough from sticking as necessary. Cut the dough into eight rectangles. 5. On each rectangle place a few spoons of the meat mixture. Fold the short ends of each roll toward the center and roll the length as you would a burrito. 6. Cut a piece of parchment to fit your air fryer basket. Place taco rolls onto the parchment and place into the air fryer basket. 7. Adjust the temperature to 180°C and air fry for 10 minutes. 8. Flip halfway through the cooking time. 9. Allow to cool 10 minutes before serving.

Greek Pork with Tzatziki Sauce

Prep time: 30 minutes | Cook time: 50 minutes | Serves 4

- Greek Pork:
- 900 g pork loin roasting joint
- Salt and black pepper, to taste
- 1 teaspoon smoked paprika
- ½ teaspoon mustard seeds
- ½ teaspoon celery salt
- 1 teaspoon fennel seeds
- 1 teaspoon chilli powder
- 1 teaspoon turmeric powder
- ½ teaspoon ground ginger
- 2 tablespoons olive oil
- 2 cloves garlic, finely chopped
- Tzatziki:
- ½ cucumber, finely chopped and squeezed
- 235 ml full-fat Greek yoghurt
- 1 garlic clove, minced
- 1 tablespoon extra-virgin olive oil
- 1 teaspoon balsamic vinegar
- 1 teaspoon minced fresh dill
- A pinch of salt

1. Toss all ingredients for Greek pork in a large mixing bowl. Toss until the meat is well coated. 2. Cook in the preheated air fryer at 180°C for 30 minutes; turn over and cook another 20 minutes. 3. Meanwhile, prepare the tzatziki by mixing all the tzatziki ingredients. Place in your refrigerator until ready to use. 4. Serve the pork sirloin roast with the chilled tzatziki on the side. Enjoy!

Italian Banger Links

Prep time: 10 minutes | Cook time: 24 minutes | Serves 4

- 1 pepper (any color), sliced
- 1 medium onion, sliced
- 1 tablespoon avocado oil
- 1 teaspoon Italian seasoning
- Sea salt and freshly ground black pepper, to taste
- 450 g Italian-seasoned banger links

1. Place the pepper and onion in a medium bowl, and toss with the avocado oil, Italian seasoning, and salt and pepper to taste. 2. Set the air fryer to 200°C. Put the vegetables in the air fryer basket and cook for 12 minutes. 3. Push the vegetables to the side of the basket and arrange the banger links in the bottom of the basket in a single layer. Spoon the vegetables over the bangers. Cook for 12 minutes, tossing halfway through, until an instant-read thermometer inserted into the banger reads 72°C.

Filipino Crispy Pork Belly

Prep time: 20 minutes | Cook time: 30 minutes | Serves 4

- 450 g pork belly
- 700 ml water
- 6 garlic cloves
- 2 tablespoons soy sauce
- 1 teaspoon coarse or flaky salt
- 1 teaspoon black pepper
- 2 bay leaves

1. Cut the pork belly into three thick chunks so it will cook more evenly. 2. Place the pork, water, garlic, soy sauce, salt, pepper, and bay leaves in the inner pot of an Instant Pot or other electric pressure cooker. Seal and cook at high pressure for 15 minutes. Let the pressure release naturally for 10 minutes, then manually release the remaining pressure. (If you do not have a

pressure cooker, place all the ingredients in a large saucepan. Cover and cook over low heat until a knife tin be easily inserted into the skin side of pork belly, about 1 hour.) Using tongs, very carefully transfer the meat to a wire rack over a rimmed baking sheet to drain and dry for 10 minutes. 3. Cut each chunk of pork belly into two long slices. Arrange the slices in the air fryer basket. Set the air fryer to 200ºC for 15 minutes, or until the fat has crisped. 4. Serve immediately.

Vietnamese "Shaking" Beef

Prep time: 30 minutes | Cook time: 4 minutes per batch | Serves 4

- Meat:
- 4 garlic cloves, minced
- 2 teaspoons soy sauce
- 2 teaspoons sugar
- 1 teaspoon toasted sesame oil
- 1 teaspoon coarse or flaky salt
- ¼ teaspoon black pepper
- 680 g flat iron or top rump steak, cut into 1-inch cubes
- Salad:
- 2 tablespoons rice vinegar or apple cider vinegar
- 2 tablespoons vegetable oil
- 1 garlic clove, minced
- 2 teaspoons sugar
- ¼ teaspoon coarse or flaky salt
- ¼ teaspoon black pepper
- ½ red onion, halved and very thinly sliced
- 1 head butterhead lettuce, leaves separated and torn into large pieces
- 120 g halved baby plum tomatoes
- 60 g fresh mint leaves
- For Serving:
- Lime wedges
- Coarse salt and freshly cracked black pepper, to taste

1. For the meat: In a small bowl, combine the garlic, soy sauce, sugar, sesame oil, salt, and pepper. Place the meat in a gallon-size resealable plastic bag. Pour the marinade over the meat. Seal and place the bag in a large bowl. Marinate for 30 minutes, or cover and refrigerate for up to 24 hours. 2. Place half the meat in the air fryer basket. Set the air fryer to 230ºC for 4 minutes, shaking the basket to redistribute the meat halfway through the cooking time. Transfer the meat to a plate (it should be medium-rare, still pink in the middle). Cover lightly with aluminium foil. Repeat to cook the remaining meat. 3. Meanwhile, for the salad: In a large bowl, whisk together the vinegar, vegetable oil, garlic, sugar, salt, and pepper. Add the onion. Stir to combine. Add the lettuce, tomatoes, and mint and toss to combine. Arrange the salad on a serving platter. 4. Arrange the cooked meat over the salad. Drizzle any accumulated juices from the plate over the meat. Serve with lime wedges, coarse salt, and cracked black pepper.

Jalapeño Popper Pork Chops

Prep time: 15 minutes | Cook time: 6 to 8 minutes | Serves 4

- 800 g bone-in, loin pork chops
- Sea salt and freshly ground black pepper, to taste
- 170 g cream cheese, at room temperature
- 110 g sliced bacon, cooked and crumbled
- 110 g Cheddar cheese, shredded
- 1 jalapeño, seeded and diced
- 1 teaspoon garlic powder

1. Cut a pocket into each pork chop, lengthwise along the side, making sure not to cut it all the way through. Season the outside of the chops with salt and pepper. 2. In a small bowl, combine the cream cheese, bacon, Cheddar cheese, jalapeño, and garlic powder. Divide this mixture among the pork chops, stuffing it into the pocket of each chop. 3. Set the air fryer to 200ºC. Place the pork chops in the air fryer basket in a single layer, working in batches if necessary. Air fry for 3 minutes. Flip the chops and cook for 3 to 5 minutes more, until an instant-read thermometer reads 64ºC. 4. Allow the chops to rest for 5 minutes, then serve warm.

Simple Beef Mince with Courgette

Prep time: 5 minutes | Cook time: 12 minutes | Serves 4

- 680 g beef mince
- 450 g chopped courgette
- 2 tablespoons extra-virgin olive oil
- 1 teaspoon dried oregano
- 1 teaspoon dried basil
- 1 teaspoon dried rosemary
- 2 tablespoons fresh chives, chopped

1. Preheat the air fryer to 200ºC. 2. In a large bowl, combine all the ingredients, except for the chives, until well blended. 3.

Place the beef and courgette mixture in the baking tray. Air fry for 12 minutes, or until the beef is browned and the courgette is tender. 4. Divide the beef and courgette mixture among four serving dishes. Top with fresh chives and serve hot.

Pork Milanese

Prep time: 10 minutes | Cook time: 12 minutes | Serves 4

- 4 (1-inch) boneless pork chops
- Fine sea salt and ground black pepper, to taste
- 2 large eggs
- 180 g pre-grated Parmesan cheese
- Chopped fresh parsley, for garnish
- Lemon slices, for serving

1. Spray the air fryer basket with avocado oil. Preheat the air fryer to 200°C. 2. Place the pork chops between 2 sheets of cling film and pound them with the flat side of a meat tenderizer until they're ¼ inch thick. Lightly season both sides of the chops with salt and pepper. 3. Lightly beat the eggs in a shallow bowl. Divide the Parmesan cheese evenly between 2 bowls and set the bowls in this order: Parmesan, eggs, Parmesan. Dredge a chop in the first bowl of Parmesan, then dip it in the eggs, and then dredge it again in the second bowl of Parmesan, making sure both sides and all edges are well coated. Repeat with the remaining chops. 4. Place the chops in the air fryer basket and air fry for 12 minutes, or until the internal temperature reaches 64°C, flipping halfway through. 5. Garnish with fresh parsley and serve immediately with lemon slices. Store leftovers in an airtight container in the refrigerator for up to 3 days. Reheat in a preheated 200°C air fryer for 5 minutes, or until warmed through.

Cheddar Bacon Burst with Spinach

Prep time: 5 minutes | Cook time: 60 minutes | Serves 8

- 30 slices bacon
- 1 tablespoon Chipotle chilli powder
- 2 teaspoons Italian seasoning
- 120 g Cheddar cheese
- 1 kg raw spinach

1. Preheat the air fryer to 190°C. 2. Weave the bacon into 15 vertical pieces and 12 horizontal pieces. Cut the extra 3 in half to fill in the rest, horizontally. 3. Season the bacon with Chipotle chilli powder and Italian seasoning. 4. Add the cheese to the bacon. 5. Add the spinach and press down to compress. 6. Tightly roll up the woven bacon. 7. Line a baking sheet with kitchen foil and add plenty of salt to it. 8. Put the bacon on top of a cooling rack and put that on top of the baking sheet. 9. Bake for 60 minutes. 10. Let cool for 15 minutes before slicing and serving.

Spice-Coated Steaks with Cucumber and Snap Pea Salad

Prep time: 15 minutes | Cook time: 15 to 20 minutes | Serves 4

- 1 (680 g) boneless rump steak, trimmed and halved crosswise
- 1½ teaspoons chilli powder
- 1½ teaspoons ground cumin
- ¾ teaspoon ground coriander
- ⅛ teaspoon cayenne pepper
- ⅛ teaspoon ground cinnamon
- 1¼ teaspoons plus ⅛ teaspoon salt, divided
- ½ teaspoon plus ⅛ teaspoon ground black pepper, divided
- 1 teaspoon plus 1½ tablespoons extra-virgin olive oil, divided
- 3 tablespoons mayonnaise
- 1½ tablespoons white wine vinegar
- 1 tablespoon minced fresh dill
- 1 small garlic clove, minced
- 230 g sugar snap peas, strings removed and cut in half on bias
- ½ cucumber, halved lengthwise and sliced thin
- 2 radishes, trimmed, halved and sliced thin
- 475 g baby rocket

1. Preheat the air fryer to 200°C. 2. In a bowl, mix chilli powder, cumin, coriander, cayenne pepper, cinnamon, 1¼ teaspoons salt and ½ teaspoon pepper until well combined. 3. Add the steaks to another bowl and pat dry with paper towels. Brush with 1 teaspoon oil and transfer to the bowl of spice mixture. Roll over to coat thoroughly. 4. Arrange the coated steaks in the air fryer basket, spaced evenly apart. Air fry for 15 to 20 minutes, or until an instant-read thermometer inserted in the thickest part of the meat registers at least 64°C. Flip halfway through to ensure even cooking. 5. Transfer the steaks to a clean work surface and wrap with aluminium foil. Let stand while preparing salad. 6. Make the salad: In a large bowl, stir together 1½ tablespoons olive oil, mayonnaise, vinegar, dill,

garlic, ⅛ teaspoon salt, and ⅛ teaspoon pepper. Add snap peas, cucumber, radishes and rocket. Toss to blend well. 7. Slice the steaks and serve with the salad.

Steak Gyro Platter

Prep time: 30 minutes | Cook time: 8 to 10 minutes | Serves 4

- 450 g bavette or skirt steak
- 1 teaspoon garlic powder
- 1 teaspoon ground cumin
- ½ teaspoon sea salt
- ½ teaspoon freshly ground black pepper
- 140 g shredded romaine lettuce
- 120 g crumbled feta cheese
- 120 g peeled and diced cucumber
- 80 g sliced red onion
- 60 g seeded and diced tomato
- 2 tablespoons pitted and sliced black olives
- Tzatziki sauce, for serving

1. Pat the steak dry with paper towels. In a small bowl, combine the garlic powder, cumin, salt, and pepper. Sprinkle this mixture all over the steak, and allow the steak to rest at room temperature for 45 minutes. 2. Preheat the air fryer to 200°C. Place the steak in the air fryer basket and air fry for 4 minutes. Flip the steak and cook 4 to 6 minutes more, until an instant-read thermometer reads 49°C at the thickest point for medium-rare (or as desired). Remove the steak from the air fryer and let it rest for 5 minutes. 3. Divide the romaine among plates. Top with the feta, cucumber, red onion, tomato, and olives.

Chicken Fried Steak with Cream Gravy

Prep time: 5 minutes | Cook time: 10 minutes | Serves 4

- 4 small thin minute steaks (about 450 g)
- ½ teaspoon salt
- ½ teaspoon freshly ground black pepper
- ¼ teaspoon garlic powder
- 1 egg, lightly beaten
- 235 g crushed pork scratchings (about 85 g)
- Cream Gravy:
- 120 ml double cream
-
- 60 g cream cheese
- 60 ml bacon fat
- 2 to 3 tablespoons water
- 2 to 3 dashes Worcestershire sauce
- Salt and freshly ground black pepper, to taste

1. Preheat Zone 1 of the air fryer to 200°C. 2. Place the steak between two sheets of parchment paper and use a meat mallet to pound to an even thickness. 3. In a small bowl, combine salt, pepper, and garlic powder. Season both sides of each steak with the mixture. 4. Place the egg in a small shallow dish and the pork rinds in another small shallow dish. Dip each steak first in the egg wash, followed by the pork rinds, pressing lightly to form an even coating. Working in batches if necessary, arrange the steaks in a single layer in Zone 1 of the air fryer basket. Air fry for 10 minutes until crispy and cooked through. 5. While the steaks are cooking, use Zone 2 of the air fryer to make the cream gravy. In a heavy-bottomed pot, warm the cream, cream cheese, and bacon fat over medium heat, whisking until smooth. Lower the heat if the mixture begins to boil. Continue whisking as you slowly add the water, 1 tablespoon at a time, until the sauce reaches the desired consistency. Season with Worcestershire sauce, salt, and pepper to taste. 6. Serve the cream gravy over the chicken fried steaks. Enjoy your delicious Chicken Fried Steak with Cream Gravy made using the Ninja Dual Zone Air Fryer!

Ritzy Skirt Steak Fajitas

Prep time: 15 minutes | Cook time: 30 minutes | Serves 4

- 2 tablespoons olive oil
- 60 ml lime juice
- 1 clove garlic, minced
- ½ teaspoon ground cumin
- ½ teaspoon hot sauce
- ½ teaspoon salt
- 2 tablespoons chopped fresh coriander
- 450 g skirt steak
- 1 onion, sliced
- 1 teaspoon chilli powder
- 1 red pepper, sliced
- 1 green pepper, sliced
- Salt and freshly ground black pepper, to taste
- 8 flour maize wraps
- Toppings:
- Shredded lettuce
- Crumbled feta or ricotta (or grated Cheddar cheese)

- Sliced black olives
- Diced tomatoes
- Sour cream
- Guacamole

1. Combine the olive oil, lime juice, garlic, cumin, hot sauce, salt and coriander in a shallow dish. Add the skirt steak and turn it over several times to coat all sides. Pierce the steak with a needle-style meat tenderizer or paring knife. Marinate the steak in the refrigerator for at least 3 hours, or overnight. When you are ready to cook, remove the steak from the refrigerator and let it sit at room temperature for 30 minutes. 2. Preheat the air fryer to 200°C. 3. Toss the onion slices with the chilli powder and a little olive oil and transfer them to the air fryer basket. Air fry for 5 minutes. Add the red and green peppers to the air fryer basket with the onions, season with salt and pepper and air fry for 8 more minutes, until the onions and peppers are soft. Transfer the vegetables to a dish and cover with aluminium foil to keep warm. 4. Put the skirt steak in the air fryer basket and pour the marinade over the top. Air fry at 200°C for 12 minutes. Flip the steak over and air fry for an additional 5 minutes. Transfer the cooked steak to a cutting board and let the steak rest for a few minutes. If the peppers and onions need to be heated, return them to the air fryer for just 1 to 2 minutes. 5. Thinly slice the steak at an angle, cutting against the grain of the steak. Serve the steak with the onions and peppers, the warm maize wraps and the fajita toppings on the side.

Italian Steak Rolls

Prep time: 30 minutes | Cook time: 9 minutes | Serves 4

- 1 tablespoon vegetable oil
- 2 cloves garlic, minced
- 2 teaspoons dried Italian seasoning
- 1 teaspoon coarse or flaky salt
- 1 teaspoon black pepper
- 450 g bavette or skirt steak, ¼ to ½ inch thick
- 1 (280 g) package frozen spinach, thawed and squeezed dry
- 120 ml diced jarred roasted red pepper
- 235 ml shredded Mozzarella cheese

1. In a large bowl, combine the oil, garlic, Italian seasoning, salt, and pepper. Whisk to combine. Add the steak to the bowl, turning to ensure the entire steak is covered with the seasonings. Cover and marinate at room temperature for 30 minutes or in the refrigerator for up to 24 hours. 2. Lay the steak on a flat surface. Spread the spinach evenly over the steak, leaving a ¼-inch border at the edge. Evenly top each steak with the red pepper and cheese. 3. Starting at a long end, roll up the steak as tightly as possible, ending seam side down. Use 2 or 3 wooden toothpicks to hold the roll together. Using a sharp knife, cut the roll in half so that it better fits in the air fryer basket. 4. Place the steak roll, seam side down, in the air fryer basket. Set the air fryer to 204°C for 9 minutes. Use a meat thermometer to ensure the steak has reached an internal temperature of 64°C. (It is critical to not overcook bavette steak, so as to not toughen the meat.) 5. Let the steak rest for 10 minutes before cutting into slices to serve.

Fruited Gammon

Prep time: 15 minutes | Cook time: 8 to 10 minutes | Serves 4

- 235 ml orange marmalade
- 48 g packed light brown sugar
- ¼ teaspoon ground cloves
- ½ teaspoon mustard powder
- 1 to 2 tablespoons oil
- 450 g cooked gammon, cut into 1-inch cubes
- 120 g canned mandarin oranges, drained and chopped

1. In a small bowl, stir together the orange marmalade, brown sugar, cloves, and mustard powder until blended. Set aside. 2. Preheat the air fryer to 160°C. Spritz a baking tray with oil. 3. Place the gammon cubes in the prepared pan. Pour the marmalade sauce over the gammon to glaze it. 4. Cook for 4 minutes. Stir and cook for 2 minutes more. 5. Add the mandarin oranges and cook for 2 to 4 minutes more until the sauce begins to thicken and the gammon is tender.

Parmesan-Crusted Pork Chops

Prep time: 5 minutes | Cook time: 12 minutes | Serves 4

- 1 large egg
- 120 g grated Parmesan cheese
- 4 (110 g) boneless pork chops
- ½ teaspoon salt
- ¼ teaspoon ground black pepper

1. Whisk egg in a medium bowl and place Parmesan in a separate medium bowl. 2. Sprinkle pork chops on both sides with salt and pepper. Dip each pork chop into egg, then press

both sides into Parmesan. 3. Place pork chops into ungreased air fryer basket. Adjust the temperature to 200°C and air fry for 12 minutes, turning chops halfway through cooking. Pork chops will be golden and have an internal temperature of at least 64°C when done. Serve warm.

Bacon-Wrapped Cheese Pork

Prep time: 10 minutes | Cook time: 20 minutes | Serves 4

- ▶ 4 (1-inch-thick) boneless pork chops
- ▶ 2 (150 g) packages Boursin cheese
- ▶ 8 slices thin-cut bacon

1. Spray the air fryer basket with avocado oil. Preheat the air fryer to 200°C. 2. Place one of the chops on a cutting board. With a sharp knife held parallel to the cutting board, make a 1-inch-wide incision on the top edge of the chop. Carefully cut into the chop to form a large pocket, leaving a ½-inch border along the sides and bottom. Repeat with the other 3 chops. 3. Snip the corner of a large resealable plastic bag to form a ¾-inch hole. Place the Boursin cheese in the bag and pipe the cheese into the pockets in the chops, dividing the cheese evenly among them. 4. Wrap 2 slices of bacon around each chop and secure the ends with toothpicks. Place the bacon-wrapped chops in the air fryer basket and cook for 10 minutes, then flip the chops and cook for another 8 to 10 minutes, until the bacon is crisp, the chops are cooked through, and the internal temperature reaches 64°C. 5. Store leftovers in an airtight container in the refrigerator for up to 3 days. Reheat in a preheated 200°C air fryer for 5 minutes, or until warmed through.

Greek Stuffed Fillet

Prep time: 10 minutes | Cook time: 10 minutes | Serves 4

- ▶ 680 g venison or beef fillet, pounded to ¼ inch thick
- ▶ 3 teaspoons fine sea salt
- ▶ 1 teaspoon ground black pepper
- ▶ 60 g creamy goat cheese
- ▶ 120 g crumbled feta cheese (about 60 g)
- ▶ 60 g finely chopped onions
- ▶ 2 cloves garlic, minced
- ▶ For Garnish/Serving (Optional):
- ▶ Yellow/American mustard
- ▶ Halved cherry tomatoes
- ▶ Extra-virgin olive oil
- ▶ Sprigs of fresh rosemary
- ▶ Lavender flowers

1. Spray the air fryer basket with avocado oil. Preheat the air fryer to 200°C. 2. Season the fillet on all sides with the salt and pepper. 3. In a medium-sized mixing bowl, combine the goat cheese, feta, onions, and garlic. Place the mixture in the center of the tenderloin. Starting at the end closest to you, tightly roll the tenderloin like a jam roll. Tie the rolled tenderloin tightly with kitchen twine. 4. Place the meat in the air fryer basket and air fry for 5 minutes. Flip the meat over and cook for another 5 minutes, or until the internal temperature reaches 57°C for medium-rare. 5. To serve, smear a line of yellow mustard on a platter, then place the meat next to it and add halved cherry tomatoes on the side, if desired. Drizzle with olive oil and garnish with rosemary sprigs and lavender flowers, if desired. 6. Best served fresh. Store leftovers in an airtight container in the fridge for 3 days. Reheat in a preheated 180°C air fryer for 4 minutes, or until heated through.

CHAPTER 5 Fish and Seafood

Crunchy Air Fried Cod Fillets

Prep time: 10 minutes | Cook time: 12 minutes | Serves 2

- 20 g panko bread crumbs
- 1 teaspoon vegetable oil
- 1 small shallot, minced
- 1 small garlic clove, minced
- ½ teaspoon minced fresh thyme
- Salt and pepper, to taste
- 1 tablespoon minced fresh parsley
- 1 tablespoon mayonnaise
- 1 large egg yolk
- ¼ teaspoon grated lemon zest, plus lemon wedges for serving
- 2 (230 g) skinless cod fillets, 1¼ inches thick
- Vegetable oil spray

1. Preheat the air fryer to 150°C. 2. Make foil sling for air fryer basket by folding 1 long sheet of aluminium foil so it is 4 inches wide. Lay sheet of foil widthwise across basket, pressing foil into and up sides of basket. Fold excess foil as needed so that edges of foil are flush with top of basket. Lightly spray the foil and basket with vegetable oil spray. 3. Toss the panko with the oil in a bowl until evenly coated. Stir in the shallot, garlic, thyme, ¼ teaspoon salt, and ⅛ teaspoon pepper. Microwave, stirring frequently, until the panko is light golden brown, about 2 minutes. Transfer to a shallow dish and let cool slightly; stir in the parsley. Whisk the mayonnaise, egg yolk, lemon zest, and ⅛ teaspoon pepper together in another bowl. 4. Pat the cod dry with paper towels and season with salt and pepper. Arrange the fillets, skinned-side down, on plate and brush tops evenly with mayonnaise mixture. (Tuck thinner tail ends of fillets under themselves as needed to create uniform pieces.) Working with 1 fillet at a time, dredge the coated side in panko mixture, pressing gently to adhere. Arrange the fillets, crumb-side up, on sling in the prepared basket, spaced evenly apart. 5. Bake for 12 to 16 minutes, using a sling to rotate fillets halfway through cooking. Using a sling, carefully remove cod from air fryer. Serve with the lemon wedges.

Tuna and Fruit Kebabs

Prep time: 15 minutes | Cook time: 8 to 12 minutes | Serves 4

- 455 g tuna steaks, cut into 1-inch cubes
- 85 g canned pineapple chunks, drained, juice reserved
- 75 g large red grapes
- 1 tablespoon honey
- 2 teaspoons grated fresh ginger
- 1 teaspoon olive oil
- Pinch cayenne pepper

1. Thread the tuna, pineapple, and grapes on 8 bamboo or 4 metal skewers that fit in the air fryer. 2. In a small bowl, whisk the honey, 1 tablespoon of reserved pineapple juice, the ginger, olive oil, and cayenne. Brush this mixture over the kebabs. Let them stand for 10 minutes. 3. Air fry the kebabs at 190°C for 8 to 12 minutes, or until the tuna reaches an internal temperature of at least 64°C on a meat thermometer, and the fruit is tender and glazed, brushing once with the remaining sauce. Discard any remaining marinade. Serve immediately.

Crispy Prawns with Coriander

Prep time: 40 minutes | Cook time: 10 minutes | Serves 4

- 455 g raw large prawns, peeled and deveined with tails on or off
- 30 g chopped fresh coriander
- Juice of 1 lime
- 35 g plain flour
- 1 egg
- 40 g bread crumbs
- Salt and freshly ground black pepper, to taste
- Cooking oil spray
- 240 ml seafood sauce

1. Place the prawns in a resealable plastic bag and add the coriander and lime juice. Seal the bag. Shake it to combine. Marinate the prawns in the refrigerator for 30 minutes. 2. Place the flour in a small bowl. 3. In another small bowl, beat the egg. 4. Place the bread crumbs in a third small bowl, season with salt and pepper, and stir to combine. 5. Insert the crisper plate

into the basket and the basket into the unit. Preheat the unit to 200°C. 6. Remove the prawns from the plastic bag. Dip each in the flour, the egg, and the bread crumbs to coat. Gently press the crumbs onto the prawns. 7. Once the unit is preheated, spray the crisper plate and the basket with cooking oil. Place the prawns in the basket. It is okay to stack them. Spray the prawns with the cooking oil. 8. Cook for 4 minutes, remove the basket and flip the prawns one at a time. Reinsert the basket to resume cooking. 10. When the cooking is complete, the prawns should be crisp. Let cool for 5 minutes. Serve with cocktail sauce.

Calamari with Hot Sauce

Prep time: 10 minutes | Cook time: 6 minutes | Serves 2

- 280 g calamari, trimmed
- 2 tablespoons hot sauce
- 1 tablespoon avocado oil

1. Slice the calamari and sprinkle with avocado oil. 2. Put the calamari in the air fryer and cook at 200°C for 3 minutes per side. 3. Then transfer the calamari in the serving plate and sprinkle with hot sauce.

Easy Scallops

Prep time: 5 minutes | Cook time: 4 minutes | Serves 2

- 12 medium sea scallops, rinsed and patted dry
- 1 teaspoon fine sea salt
- ¾ teaspoon ground black pepper, plus more for garnish
- Fresh thyme leaves, for garnish (optional)
- Avocado oil spray

1. Preheat the air fryer to 200°C. Coat the air fryer basket with avocado oil spray. 2. Place the scallops in a medium bowl and spritz with avocado oil spray. Sprinkle the salt and pepper to season. 3. Transfer the seasoned scallops to the air fryer basket, spacing them apart. You may need to work in batches to avoid overcrowding. 4. Air fry for 4 minutes, flipping the scallops halfway through, or until the scallops are firm and reach an internal temperature of just 64°C on a meat thermometer. 5. Remove from the basket and repeat with the remaining scallops. 6. Sprinkle the pepper and thyme leaves on top for garnish, if desired. Serve immediately.

Crab and Pepper Cakes

Prep time: 5 minutes | Cook time: 10 minutes | Serves 4

- 230 g jumbo lump crabmeat
- 1 tablespoon Old Bay seasoning
- 20 g bread crumbs
- 40 g diced red pepper
- 40 g diced green pepper
- 1 egg
- 60 g mayonnaise
- Juice of ½ lemon
- 1 teaspoon plain flour
- Cooking oil spray

1. Sort through the crabmeat, picking out any bits of shell or cartilage. 2. In a large bowl, stir together the Old Bay seasoning, bread crumbs, red and green peppers, egg, mayonnaise, and lemon juice. Gently stir in the crabmeat. 3. Insert the crisper plate into the basket and the basket into the unit. Preheat the unit to 190°C. 4. Form the mixture into 4 patties. Sprinkle ¼ teaspoon of flour on top of each patty. 5. Once the unit is preheated, spray the crisper plate with cooking oil. Place the crab cakes into the basket and spray them with cooking oil. 6. Cook for 10 minutes. 7. When the cooking is complete, the crab cakes will be golden brown and firm.

Asian Marinated Salmon

Prep time: 30 minutes | Cook time: 6 minutes | Serves 2

- Marinade:
- 60 ml wheat-free tamari or coconut aminos
- 2 tablespoons lime or lemon juice
- 2 tablespoons sesame oil
- 2 tablespoons powdered sweetener
- 2 teaspoons grated fresh ginger
- 2 cloves garlic, minced
- ½ teaspoon ground black pepper
- 2 (110 g) salmon fillets (about 1¼ inches thick)
- Sliced spring onions, for garnish
- Sauce (Optional):
- 60 ml beef stock
- 60 ml wheat-free tamari
- 3 tablespoons powdered sweetener
- 1 tablespoon tomato sauce
- ⅛ teaspoon guar gum or xanthan gum (optional, for

thickening)

1. Make the marinade: In a medium-sized shallow dish, stir together all the ingredients for the marinade until well combined. Place the salmon in the marinade. Cover and refrigerate for at least 2 hours or overnight. 2. Preheat the air fryer to 200°C. 3. Remove the salmon fillets from the marinade and place them in the air fryer, leaving space between them. Air fry for 6 minutes, or until the salmon is cooked through and flakes easily with a fork. 4. While the salmon cooks, make the sauce, if using: Place all the sauce ingredients except the guar gum in a medium-sized bowl and stir until well combined. Taste and adjust the sweetness to your liking. While whisking slowly, add the guar gum. Allow the sauce to thicken for 3 to 5 minutes. (The sauce tin be made up to 3 days ahead and stored in an airtight container in the fridge.) Drizzle the sauce over the salmon before serving. 5. Garnish the salmon with sliced spring onions before serving. Store leftovers in an airtight container in the fridge for up to 3 days. Reheat in a preheated 180°C air fryer for 3 minutes, or until heated through.

Tex-Mex Salmon Bowl

Prep time: 15 minutes | Cook time: 9 to 14 minutes | Serves 4

- 340 g salmon fillets, cut into 1½-inch cubes
- 1 red onion, chopped
- 1 red chilli, minced
- 1 red pepper, chopped
- 60 ml salsa
- 2 teaspoons peanut or safflower oil
- 2 tablespoons tomato juice
- 1 teaspoon chilli powder

1. Preheat the air fryer to 190°C. 2. Mix together the salmon cubes, red onion, jalapeño, red pepper, salsa, peanut oil, tomato juice, chilli powder in a medium metal bowl and stir until well incorporated. 3. Transfer the bowl to the air fryer basket and bake for 9 to 14 minutes, stirring once, or until the salmon is cooked through and the veggies are fork-tender. 4. Serve warm.

Fish Gratin

Prep time: 30 minutes | Cook time: 17 minutes | Serves 4

- 1 tablespoon avocado oil
- 455 g hake fillets
- 1 teaspoon garlic powder
- Sea salt and ground white pepper, to taste
- 2 tablespoons shallots, chopped
- 1 pepper, seeded and chopped
- 110 g cottage cheese
- 120 ml sour cream
- 1 egg, well whisked
- 1 teaspoon yellow mustard
- 1 tablespoon lime juice
- 60 g Swiss cheese, shredded

1. Brush the bottom and sides of a casserole dish with avocado oil. Add the hake fillets to the casserole dish and sprinkle with garlic powder, salt, and pepper. 2. Add the chopped shallots and peppers. 3. In a mixing bowl, thoroughly combine the Cottage cheese, sour cream, egg, mustard, and lime juice. Pour the mixture over fish and spread evenly. 4. Cook in the preheated air fryer at 190°C for 10 minutes. 5. Top with the Swiss cheese and cook an additional 7 minutes. Let it rest for 10 minutes before slicing and serving. Bon appétit!

Sesame-Crusted Tuna Steak

Prep time: 5 minutes | Cook time: 8 minutes | Serves 2

- 2 tuna steaks, 170 g each
- 1 tablespoon coconut oil, melted
- ½ teaspoon garlic powder
- 2 teaspoons white sesame seeds
- 2 teaspoons black sesame seeds

1. Brush each tuna steak with coconut oil and sprinkle with garlic powder. 2. In a large bowl, mix sesame seeds and then press each tuna steak into them, covering the steak as completely as possible. Place tuna steaks into the air fryer basket. 3. Adjust the temperature to 200°C and air fry for 8 minutes. 4. Flip the steaks halfway through the cooking time. Steaks will be well-done at 64°C internal temperature. Serve warm.

Scallops with Asparagus and Peas

Prep time: 10 minutes | Cook time: 7 to 10 minutes | Serves 4

- Cooking oil spray
- 455 g asparagus, ends trimmed, cut into 2-inch pieces
- 100 g sugar snap peas
- 455 g sea scallops
- 1 tablespoon freshly squeezed lemon juice
- 2 teaspoons extra-virgin olive oil
- ½ teaspoon dried thyme

- ▶ Salt and freshly ground black pepper, to taste

1. Insert the crisper plate into the basket and the basket into the unit. Preheat the unit to 200°C. 2. Once the unit is preheated, spray the crisper plate with cooking oil. Place the asparagus and sugar snap peas into the basket. 3. Cook for 10 minutes. 4. Meanwhile, check the scallops for a small muscle attached to the side. Pull it off and discard. In a medium bowl, toss together the scallops, lemon juice, olive oil, and thyme. Season with salt and pepper. 5. After 3 minutes, the vegetables should be just starting to get tender. Place the scallops on top of the vegetables. Reinsert the basket to resume cooking. After 3 minutes more, remove the basket and shake it. Again reinsert the basket to resume cooking. 6. When the cooking is complete, the scallops should be firm when tested with your finger and opaque in the center, and the vegetables tender. Serve immediately.

Tilapia with Pecans

Prep time: 20 minutes | Cook time: 16 minutes | Serves 5

- ▶ 2 tablespoons ground flaxseeds
- ▶ 1 teaspoon paprika
- ▶ Sea salt and white pepper, to taste
- ▶ 1 teaspoon garlic paste
- ▶ 2 tablespoons extra-virgin olive oil
- ▶ 65 g pecans, ground
- ▶ 5 tilapia fillets, sliced into halves

1. Combine the ground flaxseeds, paprika, salt, white pepper, garlic paste, olive oil, and ground pecans in a sealable freezer bag. Add the fish fillets and shake to coat well. 2. Spritz the air fryer basket with cooking spray. Cook in the preheated air fryer at 200°C for 10 minutes; turn them over and cook for 6 minutes more. Work in batches. 3. Serve with lemon wedges, if desired. Enjoy!

Almond-Crusted Fish

Prep time: 15 minutes | Cook time: 10 minutes | Serves 4

- ▶ 4 firm white fish fillets, 110g each
- ▶ 25 g breadcrumbs
- ▶ 20 g slivered almonds, crushed
- ▶ 2 tablespoons lemon juice
- ▶ ⅛ teaspoon cayenne
- ▶ Salt and pepper, to taste
- ▶ 470 g plain flour
- ▶ 1 egg, beaten with 1 tablespoon water
- ▶ Olive or vegetable oil for misting or cooking spray

1. Split fish fillets lengthwise down the center to create 8 pieces. 2. Mix breadcrumbs and almonds together and set aside. 3. Mix the lemon juice and cayenne together. Brush on all sides of fish. 4. Season fish to taste with salt and pepper. 5. Place the flour on a sheet of wax paper. 6. Roll fillets in flour, dip in egg wash, and roll in the crumb mixture. 7. Mist both sides of fish with oil or cooking spray. 8. Spray the air fryer basket and lay fillets inside. 9. Roast at 200°C for 5 minutes, turn fish over, and cook for an additional 5 minutes or until fish is done and flakes easily.

Tilapia Sandwiches with Tartar Sauce

Prep time: 8 minutes | Cook time: 17 minutes | Serves 4

- ▶ 160 g mayonnaise
- ▶ 2 tablespoons dried minced onion
- ▶ 1 dill gherkin spear, finely chopped
- ▶ 2 teaspoons gherkin juice
- ▶ ¼ teaspoon salt
- ▶ ⅛ teaspoon freshly ground black pepper
- ▶ 20 g plain flour
- ▶ 1 egg, lightly beaten
- ▶ 100 g panko bread crumbs
- ▶ 2 teaspoons lemon pepper
- ▶ 4 (170 g) tilapia fillets
- ▶ Olive oil spray
- ▶ 4 soft sub rolls
- ▶ 4 lettuce leaves

1. To make the tartar sauce, in a small bowl, whisk the mayonnaise, dried onion, pickle, gherkin juice, salt, and pepper until blended. Refrigerate while you make the fish. 2. Scoop the flour onto a plate; set aside. 3. Put the beaten egg in a medium shallow bowl. 4. On another plate, stir together the panko and lemon pepper. 5. Insert the crisper plate into the basket and the basket into the unit. Preheat the unit to 200°C. 6. Dredge the tilapia fillets in the flour, in the egg, and press into the panko mixture to coat. 7. Once the unit is preheated, spray the crisper plate with olive oil and place a baking paper liner into the basket. Place the prepared fillets on the liner in a single layer. Lightly spray the fillets with olive oil. 8. cook for 8 minutes, remove the basket, carefully flip the fillets, and spray them with more olive oil. Reinsert the basket to resume cooking. 9. When the cooking is complete, the fillets should be golden and crispy

and a food thermometer should register 64°C. Place each cooked fillet in a sub roll, top with a little bit of tartar sauce and lettuce, and serve.

Crustless Prawn Quiche

Prep time: 15 minutes | Cook time: 20 minutes | Serves 2

- Vegetable oil
- 4 large eggs
- 120 ml single cream
- 110 g raw prawns, chopped
- 120 g shredded Parmesan or Swiss cheese
- 235 g chopped spring onions
- 1 teaspoon sweet smoked paprika
- 1 teaspoon Herbes de Provence
- 1 teaspoon black pepper
- ½ to 1 teaspoon kosher or coarse sea salt

1. Generously grease a baking pan with vegetable oil. (Be sure to grease the pan well, the proteins in eggs stick something fierce. Alternatively, line the bottom of the pan with baking paper cut to fit and spray the baking paper and sides of the pan generously with vegetable oil spray.) 2. In a large bowl, beat together the eggs and single cream. Add the prawns, 90 g of the cheese, the spring onions, paprika, Herbes de Provence, pepper, and salt. Stir with a fork to thoroughly combine. Pour the egg mixture into the prepared pan. 3. Place the pan in the air fryer basket. Set the air fryer to 150°C for 20 minutes. After 17 minutes, sprinkle the remaining 30 g cheese on top and cook for the remaining 3 minutes, or until the cheese has melted, the eggs are set, and a toothpick inserted into the center comes out clean. 4. Serve the quiche warm or at room temperature.

Almond Catfish

Prep time: 10 minutes | Cook time: 12 minutes | Serves 4

- 900 g catfish fillet
- 25 g almond flour
- 2 eggs, beaten
- 1 teaspoon salt
- 1 teaspoon avocado oil

1. Sprinkle the catfish fillet with salt and dip in the eggs. 2. Then coat the fish in the almond flour and put in the air fryer basket. Sprinkle the fish with avocado oil. 3. Cook the fish for 6 minutes per side at 190°C.

Baked Monkfish

Prep time: 20 minutes | Cook time: 12 minutes | Serves 2

- 2 teaspoons olive oil
- 100 g celery, sliced
- 2 peppers, sliced
- 1 teaspoon dried thyme
- ½ teaspoon dried marjoram
- ½ teaspoon dried rosemary
- 2 monkfish fillets
- 1 tablespoon coconut aminos, or tamari
- 2 tablespoons lime juice
- Coarse salt and ground black pepper, to taste
- 1 teaspoon cayenne pepper
- 90 g Kalamata olives, pitted and sliced

1. In a nonstick frying pan, heat the olive oil for 1 minute. Once hot, sauté the celery and peppers until tender, about 4 minutes. Sprinkle with thyme, marjoram, and rosemary and set aside. 2. Toss the fish fillets with the coconut aminos, lime juice, salt, black pepper, and cayenne pepper. Place the fish fillets in the lightly greased air fryer basket and bake at 200°C for 8 minutes. 3. Turn them over, add the olives, and cook an additional 4 minutes. Serve with the sautéed vegetables on the side. Bon appétit!

Snapper Scampi

Prep time: 5 minutes | Cook time: 8 to 10 minutes | Serves 4

- 4 skinless snapper or arctic char fillets, 170 g each
- 1 tablespoon olive oil
- 3 tablespoons lemon juice, divided
- ½ teaspoon dried basil
- Pinch salt
- Freshly ground black pepper, to taste
- 2 tablespoons butter
- 2 cloves garlic, minced

1. Rub the fish fillets with olive oil and 1 tablespoon of the lemon juice. Sprinkle with the basil, salt, and pepper, and place in the air fryer basket. 2. Air fry the fish at 190°C for 7 to 8 minutes or until the fish just flakes when tested with a fork. Remove the fish from the basket and put on a serving plate. Cover to keep warm. 3. In a baking pan, combine the butter, remaining 2 tablespoons lemon juice, and garlic. Bake in the air fryer for 1 to 2 minutes or until the garlic is sizzling. Pour this

mixture over the fish and serve.

Panko-Crusted Fish Fingers

Prep time: 10 minutes | Cook time: 15 minutes | Serves 4

- Tartar Sauce:
- 470 ml mayonnaise
- 2 tablespoons dill gherkin relish
- 1 tablespoon dried minced onions
- Fish Fingers:
- Olive or vegetable oil, for spraying
- 455 g tilapia fillets
- 40 g plain flour
- 60 g panko bread crumbs
- 2 tablespoons Creole seasoning
- 2 teaspoons garlic granules
- 1 teaspoon onion powder
- ½ teaspoon salt
- ¼ teaspoon freshly ground black pepper
- 1 large egg

Make the Tartar Sauce: 1. In a small bowl, whisk together the mayonnaise, gherkin relish, and onions. Cover with cling film and refrigerate until ready to serve. You tin make this sauce ahead of time; the flavours will intensify as it chills. Make the Fish Fingers: 2. Preheat the air fryer to 180°C. Line the air fryer basket with baking paper and spray lightly with oil. 3. Cut the fillets into equal-size sticks and place them in a zip-top plastic bag. 4. Add the flour to the bag, seal, and shake well until evenly coated. 5. In a shallow bowl, mix together the bread crumbs, Creole seasoning, garlic, onion powder, salt, and black pepper. 6. In a small bowl, whisk the egg. 7. Dip the fish fingers in the egg, then dredge in the bread crumb mixture until completely coated. 8. Place the fish fingers in the prepared basket. You may need to work in batches, depending on the size of your air fryer. Do not overcrowd. Spray lightly with oil. 9. Cook for 12 to 15 minutes, or until browned and cooked through. Serve with the tartar sauce.

Friday Night Fish-Fry

Prep time: 10 minutes | Cook time: 10 minutes | Serves 4

- 1 large egg
- 25 g powdered Parmesan cheese
- 1 teaspoon smoked paprika
- ¼ teaspoon celery salt
- ¼ teaspoon ground black pepper
- 4 cod fillets, 110 g each
- Chopped fresh oregano or parsley, for garnish (optional)
- Lemon slices, for serving (optional)

1. Spray the air fryer basket with avocado oil. Preheat the air fryer to 200°C. 2. Crack the egg in a shallow bowl and beat it lightly with a fork. Combine the Parmesan cheese, paprika, celery salt, and pepper in a separate shallow bowl. 3. One at a time, dip the fillets into the egg, then dredge them in the Parmesan mixture. Using your hands, press the Parmesan onto the fillets to form a nice crust. As you finish, place the fish in the air fryer basket. 4. Air fry the fish in the air fryer for 10 minutes, or until it is cooked through and flakes easily with a fork. Garnish with fresh oregano or parsley and serve with lemon slices, if desired. 5. Store leftovers in an airtight container in the refrigerator for up to 3 days. Reheat in a preheated 200°C air fryer for 5 minutes, or until warmed through.

Parmesan Mackerel with Coriander

Prep time: 10 minutes | Cook time: 7 minutes | Serves 2

- 340 g mackerel fillet
- 60 g Parmesan, grated
- 1 teaspoon ground coriander
- 1 tablespoon olive oil

1. Sprinkle the mackerel fillet with olive oil and put it in the air fryer basket. 2. Top the fish with ground coriander and Parmesan. 3. Cook the fish at 200°C for 7 minutes.

Simple Cheesy Shrimps

Prep time: 10 minutes | Cook time: 16 minutes | Serves 4 to 6

- 160 g grated Parmesan cheese
- 4 minced garlic cloves
- 1 teaspoon onion powder
- ½ teaspoon oregano
- 1 teaspoon basil
- 1 teaspoon ground black pepper
- 2 tablespoons olive oil
- 900 g cooked large shrimps, peeled and deveined
- Lemon wedges, for topping
- Cooking spray

1. Preheat the air fryer to 180°C 2.Spritz the air fryer basket

with cooking spray 3.Combine all the ingredients, except for the shrimps, in a large bowl 4.Stir to mix well 5.Dunk the shrimps in the mixture and toss to coat well 6.Shake the excess off 7.Arrange the shrimps in the preheated air fryer 8.Air fry for 8 minutes or until opaque 9.Flip the shrimps halfway through 10.You may need to work in batches to avoid overcrowding 11.Transfer the cooked shrimps on a large plate and squeeze the lemon wedges over before serving.

CHAPTER 6 Snacks and Starters

Courgette Feta Roulades

Prep time: 10 minutes | Cook time: 10 minutes | Serves 6

- 55 g feta cheese
- 1 garlic clove, minced
- 2 tablespoons fresh basil, minced
- 1 tablespoon capers, minced
- ⅛ teaspoon salt
- ⅛ teaspoon red pepper flakes
- 1 tablespoon lemon juice
- 2 medium courgette
- 12 cocktail sticks

1. Preheat the air fryer to 180°C. (If using a grill attachment, make sure it is inside the air fryer during preheating.) 2. In a small bowl, combine the feta cheese, garlic, basil, capers, salt, red pepper flakes, and lemon juice. 3. Slice the courgette into ⅛-inch strips lengthwise. (Each courgette should yield around 6 strips.) 4. Spread 1 tablespoon of the cheese filling onto each slice of courgette, then roll it up and secure it with a cocktail stick through the middle. 5. Place the courgette roulades into the air fryer basket in a single layer, making sure that they don't touch each other. 6. Bake or grill in the air fryer for 10 minutes. 7. Remove the courgette roulades from the air fryer and gently remove the cocktail sticks before serving.

Mexican Potato Skins

Prep time: 10 minutes | Cook time: 55 minutes | Serves 6

- Olive oil
- 6 medium russet potatoes or Maris Piper potatoes, scrubbed
- Salt and freshly ground black pepper, to taste
- 260 g fat-free refried black beans
- 1 tablespoon taco seasoning
- 120 g salsa
- 80 g low-fat shredded Cheddar cheese

1. Spray the air fryer basket lightly with olive oil. 2. Spray the potatoes lightly with oil and season with salt and pepper. Pierce each potato a few times with a fork. 3. Place the potatoes in the air fryer basket. Air fry at 200°C until fork-tender, 30 to 40 minutes. The cooking time will depend on the size of the potatoes. You tin cook the potatoes in the microwave or a standard oven, but they won't get the same lovely crispy skin they will get in the air fryer. 4. While the potatoes are cooking, in a small bowl, mix together the beans and taco seasoning. Set aside until the potatoes are cool enough to handle. 5. Cut each potato in half lengthwise. Scoop out most of the insides, leaving about ¼ inch in the skins so the potato skins hold their shape. 6. Season the insides of the potato skins with salt and black pepper. Lightly spray the insides of the potato skins with oil. You may need to cook them in batches. 7. Place them into the air fryer basket, skin-side down, and air fry until crisp and golden, 8 to 10 minutes. 8. Transfer the skins to a work surface and spoon ½ tablespoon of seasoned refried black beans into each one. Top each with 2 teaspoons salsa and 1 tablespoon shredded Cheddar cheese. 9. Place filled potato skins in the air fryer basket in a single layer. Lightly spray with oil. 10. Air fry until the cheese is melted and bubbly, 2 to 3 minutes.

Spiced Roasted Cashews

Prep time: 5 minutes | Cook time: 10 minutes | Serves 4

- 250 g raw cashews
- 2 tablespoons olive oil
- ¼ teaspoon salt
- ¼ teaspoon chilli powder
- ⅛ teaspoon garlic powder
- ⅛ teaspoon smoked paprika

1. Preheat the air fryer to 180°C. 2. In a large bowl, toss all of the ingredients together. 3. Pour the cashews into the air fryer basket and roast them for 5 minutes. Shake the basket, then cook for 5 minutes more. 4. Serve immediately.

Chilli-brined Fried Calamari

Prep time: 20 minutes | Cook time: 8 minutes | Serves 2

- 1 (227 g) jar sweet or hot pickled cherry peppers
- 227 g calamari bodies and tentacles, bodies cut into ½-inch-wide rings
- 1 lemon
- 200 g plain flour

- Rock salt and freshly ground black pepper, to taste
- 3 large eggs, lightly beaten
- Cooking spray
- 120 ml mayonnaise
- 1 teaspoon finely chopped rosemary
- 1 garlic clove, minced

1. Drain the pickled pepper brine into a large bowl and tear the peppers into bite-size strips. Add the pepper strips and calamari to the brine and let stand in the refrigerator for 20 minutes or up to 2 hours. 2. Grate the lemon zest into a large bowl then whisk in the flour and season with salt and pepper. Dip the calamari and pepper strips in the egg, then toss them in the flour mixture until fully coated. Spray the calamari and peppers liberally with cooking spray, then transfer half to the air fryer. Air fry at 200°C, shaking the basket halfway into cooking, until the calamari is fully cooked and golden, about 8 minutes. Transfer to a plate and repeat with the remaining pieces. 3. In a small bowl, whisk together the mayonnaise, rosemary, and garlic. Squeeze half the zested lemon to get 1 tablespoon of juice and stir it into the sauce. Season with salt and pepper. Cut the remaining zested lemon half into 4 small wedges and serve alongside the calamari, peppers, and sauce.

Spinach and Crab Meat Cups

Prep time: 10 minutes | Cook time: 10 minutes | Makes 30 cups

- 1 (170 g) tin crab meat, drained to yield 80 g meat
- 30 g frozen spinach, thawed, drained, and chopped
- 1 clove garlic, minced
- 84 g grated Parmesan cheese
- 3 tablespoons plain yoghurt
- ¼ teaspoon lemon juice
- ½ teaspoon Worcestershire sauce
- 30 mini frozen filo shells, thawed
- Cooking spray

1. Preheat the air fryer to 200°C. 2. Remove any bits of shell that might remain in the crab meat. 3. Mix the crab meat, spinach, garlic, and cheese together. 4. Stir in the yoghurt, lemon juice, and Worcestershire sauce and mix well. 5. Spoon a teaspoon of filling into each filo shell. 6. Spray the air fryer basket with cooking spray and arrange half the shells in the basket. Air fry for 5 minutes. Repeat with the remaining shells. 7. Serve immediately.

Crispy Green Bean Fries with Lemon-Yoghurt Sauce

Prep time: 5 minutes | Cook time: 5 minutes | Serves 4

- French beans:
- 1 egg
- 2 tablespoons water
- 1 tablespoon wholemeal flour
- ¼ teaspoon paprika
- ½ teaspoon garlic powder
- ½ teaspoon salt
- 25 g wholemeal breadcrumbs
- 227 g whole French beans
- Lemon-Yoghurt Sauce:
- 120 ml non-fat plain Greek yoghurt
- 1 tablespoon lemon juice
- ¼ teaspoon salt
- ⅛ teaspoon cayenne pepper

Make the French beans: 1. Preheat the air fryer to 190°C. 2. In a medium shallow dish, beat together the egg and water until frothy. 3. In a separate medium shallow dish, whisk together the flour, paprika, garlic powder, and salt, then mix in the breadcrumbs. 4. Spray the bottom of the air fryer with cooking spray. 5. Dip each green bean into the egg mixture, then into the bread crumb mixture, coating the outside with the crumbs. Place the French beans in a single layer in the bottom of the air fryer basket. 6. Fry in the air fryer for 5 minutes, or until the breading is golden. Make the Lemon-Yoghurt Sauce: 7. In a small bowl, combine the yoghurt, lemon juice, salt, and cayenne. 8. Serve the green bean fries alongside the lemon-yoghurt sauce as a snack or starter.

Rosemary-Garlic Shoestring Fries

Prep time: 5 minutes | Cook time: 18 minutes | Serves 2

- 1 large russet potatoes or Maris Piper potato (about 340 g), scrubbed clean, and julienned
- 1 tablespoon mixed vegetables oil
- Leaves from 1 sprig fresh rosemary
- Rock salt and freshly ground black pepper, to taste
- 1 garlic clove, thinly sliced
- Flaky sea salt, for serving

1. Preheat the air fryer to 200°C. 2. Place the julienned potatoes in a large colander and rinse under cold running water until the water runs clear. Spread the potatoes out on a double layer of

kitchen roll and pat dry. 3. In a large bowl, combine the potatoes, oil, and rosemary. Season with rock salt and pepper and toss to coat evenly. Place the potatoes in the air fryer and air fry for 18 minutes, shaking the basket every 5 minutes and adding the garlic in the last 5 minutes of cooking, or until the fries are golden and crisp. 4. Transfer the fries to a plate and sprinkle with flaky sea salt while they're hot. Serve immediately.

Cheesy Steak Fries

Prep time: 5 minutes | Cook time: 20 minutes | Serves 5

- 1 (794 g) bag frozen chunky chips
- Cooking spray
- Salt and pepper, to taste
- 120 ml beef gravy
- 90 g shredded mozzarella cheese cheese
- 2 spring onions, green parts only, chopped

1. Preheat the air fryer to 200°C. 2. Place the frozen chunky chips in the air fryer. Air fry for 10 minutes. Shake the basket and spritz the fries with cooking spray. Sprinkle with salt and pepper. Air fry for an additional 8 minutes. 3. Pour the beef gravy into a medium, microwave-safe bowl. Microwave for 30 seconds, or until the gravy is warm. 4. Sprinkle the fries with the cheese. Air fry for an additional 2 minutes, until the cheese is melted. 5. Transfer the fries to a serving dish. Drizzle the fries with gravy and sprinkle the spring onions on top for a green garnish. Serve.

Roasted Mushrooms with Garlic

Prep time: 3 minutes | Cook time: 22 to 27 minutes | Serves 4

- 16 garlic cloves, peeled
- 2 teaspoons olive oil, divided
- 16 button mushrooms
- ½ teaspoon dried marjoram
- ⅛ teaspoon freshly ground black pepper
- 1 tablespoon white wine or low-salt mixed vegetables broth

1. In a baking pan, mix the garlic with 1 teaspoon of olive oil. Roast in the air fryer at 180°C for 12 minutes. 2. Add the mushrooms, marjoram, and pepper. Stir to coat. Drizzle with the remaining 1 teaspoon of olive oil and the white wine. 3. Return to the air fryer and roast for 10 to 15 minutes more, or until the mushrooms and garlic cloves are tender. Serve.

Easy Spiced Nuts

Prep time: 5 minutes | Cook time: 25 minutes | Makes 3 L

- 1 egg white, lightly beaten
- 48 g sugar
- 1 teaspoon salt
- ½ teaspoon cinnamon powder
- ¼ teaspoon ground cloves
- ¼ teaspoon ground allspice
- Pinch ground cayenne pepper
- 100 g pecan halves
- 135 g cashews
- 140 g almonds

1. Combine the egg white with the sugar and spices in a bowl. 2. Preheat the air fryer to 150°C. 3. Spray or brush the air fryer basket with mixed vegetables oil. Toss the nuts together in the spiced egg white and transfer the nuts to the air fryer basket. 4. Air fry for 25 minutes, stirring the nuts in the basket a few times during the cooking process. Taste the nuts (carefully because they will be very hot) to see if they are crunchy and nicely toasted. Air fry for a few more minutes if necessary. 5. Serve warm or cool to at room temperature and store in an airtight container for up to two weeks.

Spiralized Potato Nest with Tomato Tomato Ketchup

Prep time: 10 minutes | Cook time: 15 minutes | Serves 2

- 1 large russet potatoes or Maris Piper potato (about 340 g)
- 2 tablespoons mixed vegetables oil
- 1 tablespoon hot smoked paprika
- ½ teaspoon garlic powder
- Rock salt and freshly ground black pepper, to taste
- 120 ml canned chopped tomatoes
- 2 tablespoons apple cider vinegar
- 1 tablespoon dark brown sugar
- 1 tablespoon Worcestershire sauce
- 1 teaspoon mild hot sauce

1. Using a spiralizer, spiralize the potato, then place in a large colander. (If you don't have a spiralizer, cut the potato into thin ⅛-inch-thick matchsticks.) Rinse the potatoes under cold running water until the water runs clear. Spread the potatoes out on a double layer of kitchen roll and pat completely dry. 2.

In a large bowl, combine the potatoes, oil, paprika, and garlic powder. Season with salt and pepper and toss to combine. Transfer the potatoes to the air fryer and air fry at 200°C until the potatoes are browned and crisp, 15 minutes, shaking the basket halfway through. 3. Meanwhile, in a small blender, purée the tomatoes, vinegar, brown sugar, Worcestershire sauce, and hot sauce until smooth. Pour into a small saucepan or frying pan and simmer medium heat until reduced by half, 3 to 5 minutes. Pour the homemade tomato ketchup into a bowl and let cool. 4. Remove the spiralized potato nest from the air fryer and serve hot with the tomato ketchup.

Air Fried Spicy Olives

Prep time: 10 minutes | Cook time: 5 minutes | Serves 4

- 340 g pitted black extra-large olives
- 30 g plain flour
- 120 g panko breadcrumbs
- 2 teaspoons dried thyme
- 1 teaspoon red pepper flakes
- 1 teaspoon smoked paprika
- 1 egg beaten with 1 tablespoon water
- Vegetable oil for spraying

1. Preheat the air fryer to 200°C 2.Drain the olives and place them on a paper towel–lined plate to dry 3.Put the flour on a plate 4.Combine the panko, thyme, red pepper flakes, and paprika on a separate plate 5.Dip an olive in the flour, shaking off any excess, then coat with egg mixture 6.Dredge the olive in the panko mixture, pressing to make the crumbs adhere, and place the breaded olive on a platter 7.Repeat with the remaining olives 8.Spray the olives with oil and place them in a single layer in the air fryer basket 9.Work in batches if necessary so as not to overcrowd the basket 10.Air fry for 5 minutes until the breading is browned and crispy 11.Serve warm

Goat Cheese and Garlic Crostini

Prep time: 3 minutes | Cook time: 5 minutes | Serves 4

- 1 wholemeal baguette
- 60 ml olive oil
- 2 garlic cloves, minced
- 113 g goat cheese
- 2 tablespoons fresh basil, minced

1. Preheat the air fryer to 190°C. 2. Cut the baguette into ½-inch-thick slices. 3. In a small bowl, mix together the olive oil and garlic, then brush it over one side of each slice of bread. 4. Place the olive-oil-coated bread in a single layer in the air fryer basket and bake for 5 minutes. 5. Meanwhile, in a small bowl, mix together the goat cheese and basil. 6. Remove the toast from the air fryer, then spread a thin layer of the goat cheese mixture over the top of each piece and serve.

Lebanese Muhammara

Prep time: 15 minutes | Cook time: 15 minutes | Serves 6

- 2 large red peppers
- 60 ml plus 2 tablespoons extra-virgin olive oil
- 85 g walnut halves
- 1 tablespoon agave syrup or honey
- 1 teaspoon fresh lemon juice
- 1 teaspoon cumin powder
- 1 teaspoon rock salt
- 1 teaspoon red pepper flakes
- Raw mixed vegetables (such as cucumber, carrots, sliced courgette, or cauliflower) or toasted pitta bread chips, for serving

1. Drizzle the peppers with 2 tablespoons of the olive oil and place in the air fryer basket. Set the air fryer to 200°C for 10 minutes. 2. Add the walnuts to the basket, arranging them around the peppers. Set the air fryer to 200°C for 5 minutes. 3. Remove the peppers, seal in a a resealable plastic bag, and let rest for 5 to 10 minutes. Transfer the walnuts to a plate and set aside to cool down. 4. Place the softened peppers, walnuts, agave, lemon juice, cumin, salt, and ½ teaspoon of the pepper flakes blend in a food processor until smooth. 5. Transfer the dip to a serving bowl and create an indentation in the middle. Pour the remaining 60 ml olive oil into the indentation. Garnish the dip with the remaining ½ teaspoon pepper flakes. 6. Serve with mixed vegetables or toasted pitta bread chips.

Crispy Breaded Beef Cubes

Prep time: 10 minutes | Cook time: 12 to 16 minutes | Serves 4

- 450 g sirloin tip, cut into 1-inch cubes
- 240 ml cheese pasta sauce
- 355 g soft breadcrumbs
- 2 tablespoons olive oil
- ½ teaspoon dried marjoram

1. Preheat the air fryer to 180°C. 2. In a medium-sized bowl, toss the beef with the pasta sauce to coat. 3. In a shallow dish,

combine the breadcrumbs, oil, and marjoram, and mix well. Drop the beef cubes, one at a time, into the bread crumb mixture to coat thoroughly. 4. Air fry the beef in two batches for 6 to 8 minutes, shaking the basket once during cooking time, until the beef is at least 63°C and the outside is crisp and brown. 5. Serve hot.

Greek Yoghurt Devilled Eggs

Prep time: 15 minutes | Cook time: 15 minutes | Serves 4

- 4 eggs
- 60 ml non-fat plain Greek yoghurt
- 1 teaspoon chopped fresh fresh dill
- ⅛ teaspoon salt
- ⅛ teaspoon paprika
- ⅛ teaspoon garlic powder
- Chopped fresh parsley, for garnish

1. Preheat the air fryer to 130°C. 2. Place the eggs in a single layer in the air fryer basket and cook for 15 minutes. 3. Quickly remove the eggs from the air fryer and place them into a cold water bath. Let the eggs cool in the water for 10 minutes before removing and peeling them. 4. After peeling the eggs, cut them in half. 5. Spoon the yolk into a small bowl. Add the yoghurt, fresh dill, salt, paprika, and garlic powder and mix until smooth. 6. Spoon or pipe the yolk mixture into the halved egg whites. Serve with a sprinkle of fresh parsley on top.

Pepperoni Pizza Dip

Prep time: 10 minutes | Cook time: 10 minutes | Serves 6

- 170 g soft white cheese
- 85 g shredded Italian cheese blend
- 60 ml soured cream
- 1½ teaspoons dried Italian seasoning
- ¼ teaspoon garlic salt
- ¼ teaspoon onion powder
- 165 g pizza sauce
- 42 g sliced miniature pepperoni
- 400 g sliced black olives
- 1 tablespoon thinly sliced spring onion
- Cut-up raw mixed vegetables, toasted baguette slices, pitta chips, or tortilla chips, for serving

1. In a small bowl, combine the soft white cheese, 28 g of the shredded cheese, the soured cream, Italian seasoning, garlic salt, and onion powder. Stir until smooth and the ingredients are well blended. 2. Spread the mixture in a baking pan. Top with the pizza sauce, spreading to the edges. Sprinkle with the remaining 56 g shredded cheese. Arrange the pepperoni slices on top of the cheese. Top with the black olives and green onion. 3. Place the pan in the air fryer basket. Set the air fryer to 180°C for 10 minutes, or until the pepperoni is beginning to brown on the edges and the cheese is bubbly and lightly browned. 4. Let stand for 5 minutes before serving with mixed vegetables, toasted baguette slices, pitta chips, or tortilla chips.

Mixed Vegetables Pot Stickers

Prep time: 12 minutes | Cook time: 11 to 18 minutes | Makes 12 pot stickers

- 70 g shredded red cabbage
- 25 g chopped button mushrooms
- 35 g grated carrot
- 2 tablespoons minced onion
- 2 garlic cloves, minced
- 2 teaspoons grated fresh ginger
- 12 gyoza/pot sticker wrappers
- 2½ teaspoons olive oil, divided

1. In a baking pan, combine the red cabbage, mushrooms, carrot, onion, garlic, and ginger. Add 1 tablespoon of water. Place in the air fryer and air fry at 190°C for 3 to 6 minutes, until the mixed vegetables are crisp-tender. Drain and set aside. 2. Working one at a time, place the pot sticker wrappers on a work surface. Top each wrapper with a scant 1 tablespoon of the filling. Fold half of the wrapper over the other half to form a half circle. Dab one edge with water and press both edges together. 3. To another pan, add 1¼ teaspoons of olive oil. Put half of the pot stickers, seam-side up, in the pan. Air fry for 5 minutes, or until the bottoms are light golden. Add 1 tablespoon of water and return the pan to the air fryer. 4. Air fry for 4 to 6 minutes more, or until hot. Repeat with the remaining pot stickers, remaining 1¼ teaspoons of oil, and another tablespoon of water. Serve immediately.

Greek Potato Skins with Olives and Feta

Prep time: 5 minutes | Cook time: 45 minutes | Serves 4

- 2 russet potatoes or Maris Piper potatoes
- 3 tablespoons olive oil, divided, plus more for drizzling (optional)
- 1 teaspoon rock salt, divided

- ¼ teaspoon black pepper
- 2 tablespoons fresh coriander, chopped, plus more for serving
- 60 g Kalamata olives, diced
- 60 g crumbled feta cheese
- Chopped fresh parsley, for garnish (optional)

1. Preheat the air fryer to 190°C. 2. Using a fork, poke 2 to 3 holes in the potatoes, then coat each with about ½ tablespoon olive oil and ½ teaspoon salt. 3. Place the potatoes into the air fryer basket and bake for 30 minutes. 4. Remove the potatoes from the air fryer, and slice in half. Using a spoon, scoop out the flesh of the potatoes, leaving a ½-inch layer of potato inside the skins, and set the skins aside. 5. In a medium-sized bowl, combine the scooped potato middles with the remaining 2 tablespoons of olive oil, ½ teaspoon of salt, black pepper, and coriander. Mix until well combined. 6. Divide the potato filling into the now-empty potato skins, spreading it evenly over them. Top each potato with a tablespoon each of the olives and feta cheese. 7. Place the loaded potato skins back into the air fryer and bake for 15 minutes. 8. Serve with additional chopped coriander or parsley and a drizzle of olive oil, if desired.

Air Fried Pot Stickers

Prep time: 10 minutes | Cook time: 18 to 20 minutes | Makes 30 pot stickers

- 35 g finely chopped cabbage
- 30 g finely chopped red pepper
- 2 spring onions, finely chopped
- 1 egg, beaten
- 2 tablespoons cocktail sauce
- 2 teaspoons low-salt soy sauce
- 30 wonton wrappers
- 1 tablespoon water, for brushing the wrappers

1. Preheat the air fryer to 180°C. 2. In a small bowl, combine the cabbage, pepper, spring onions, egg, cocktail sauce, and soy sauce, and mix well. 3. Put about 1 teaspoon of the mixture in the centre of each wonton wrapper. Fold the wrapper in half, covering the filling; dampen the edges with water, and seal. You tin crimp the edges of the wrapper with your fingers, so they look like the pot stickers you get in restaurants. Brush them with water. 4. Place the pot stickers in the air fryer basket and air fry in 2 batches for 9 to 10 minutes, or until the pot stickers are hot and the bottoms are lightly browned. 5. Serve hot.

CHAPTER 7 Vegetables and Sides

Crispy Courgette Sticks

Prep time: 5 minutes | Cook time: 14 minutes | Serves 4

- 2 small courgette, cut into 2-inch × ½-inch sticks
- 3 tablespoons chickpea flour
- 2 teaspoons arrowroot (or cornflour)
- ½ teaspoon garlic granules
- ¼ teaspoon sea salt
- ⅛ teaspoon freshly ground black pepper
- 1 tablespoon water
- Cooking spray

1. Preheat the air fryer to 200°C. 2. Combine the courgette sticks with the chickpea flour, arrowroot, garlic granules, salt, and pepper in a medium bowl and toss to coat. Add the water and stir to mix well. 3. Spritz the air fryer basket with cooking spray and spread out the courgette sticks in the basket. Mist the courgette sticks with cooking spray. 4. Air fry for 14 minutes, shaking the basket halfway through, or until the courgette sticks are crispy and nicely browned. 5. Serve warm.

Parmesan-Thyme Butternut Marrow

Prep time: 15 minutes | Cook time: 20 minutes | Serves 4

- 350 g butternut marrow, cubed into 1-inch pieces (approximately 1 medium)
- 2 tablespoons olive oil
- ¼ teaspoon salt
- ¼ teaspoon garlic powder
- ¼ teaspoon black pepper
- 1 tablespoon fresh thyme
- 20 g grated Parmesan

1. Preheat the air fryer to 180°C. 2. In a large bowl, combine the cubed marrow with the olive oil, salt, garlic powder, pepper, and thyme until the marrow is well coated. 3. Pour this mixture into the air fryer basket, and roast for 10 minutes. Stir and roast another 8 to 10 minutes more. 4. Remove the marrow from the air fryer and toss with freshly grated Parmesan before serving.

Garlic and Thyme Tomatoes

Prep time: 10 minutes | Cook time: 15 minutes | Serves 2 to 4

- 4 plum tomatoes
- 1 tablespoon olive oil
- Salt and freshly ground black pepper, to taste
- 1 clove garlic, minced
- ½ teaspoon dried thyme

1. Preheat the air fryer to 200°C. 2. Cut the tomatoes in half and scoop out the seeds and any pithy parts with your fingers. Place the tomatoes in a bowl and toss with the olive oil, salt, pepper, garlic and thyme. 3. Transfer the tomatoes to the air fryer, cut side up. Air fry for 15 minutes. The edges should just start to brown. Let the tomatoes cool to an edible temperature for a few minutes and then use in pastas, on top of crostini, or as an accompaniment to any poultry, meat or fish.

Parmesan and Herb Sweet Potatoes

Prep time: 10 minutes | Cook time: 18 minutes | Serves 4

- 2 large sweet potatoes, peeled and cubed
- 65 ml olive oil
- 1 teaspoon dried rosemary
- ½ teaspoon salt
- 2 tablespoons shredded Parmesan

1. Preheat the air fryer to 180°C. 2. In a large bowl, toss the sweet potatoes with the olive oil, rosemary, and salt. 3. Pour the potatoes into the air fryer basket and roast for 10 minutes, then stir the potatoes and sprinkle the Parmesan over the top. Continue roasting for 8 minutes more. 4. Serve hot and enjoy.

Cheesy Loaded Broccoli

Prep time: 10 minutes | Cook time: 10 minutes | Serves 2

- 215 g fresh broccoli florets
- 1 tablespoon coconut oil
- ¼ teaspoon salt
- 120 g shredded sharp Cheddar cheese
- 60 g sour cream
- 4 slices cooked sugar-free bacon, crumbled
- 1 medium spring onion, trimmed and sliced on the

bias

1. Place broccoli into ungreased air fryer basket, drizzle with coconut oil, and sprinkle with salt. Adjust the temperature to 180ºC and roast for 8 minutes. Shake basket three times during cooking to avoid burned spots. 2. Sprinkle broccoli with Cheddar and cook for 2 additional minutes. When done, cheese will be melted and broccoli will be tender. 3. Serve warm in a large serving dish, topped with sour cream, crumbled bacon, and spring onion slices.

Courgette Balls

Prep time: 5 minutes | Cook time: 10 minutes | Serves 4

- 4 courgettes
- 1 egg
- 45 g grated Parmesan cheese
- 1 tablespoon Italian herbs
- 75 g grated coconut

1. Thinly grate the courgettes and dry with a cheesecloth, ensuring to remove all the moisture. 2. In a bowl, combine the courgettes with the egg, Parmesan, Italian herbs, and grated coconut, mixing well to incorporate everything. Using the hands, mould the mixture into balls. 3. Preheat the air fryer to 200ºC. 4. Lay the courgette balls in the air fryer basket and air fry for 10 minutes. 5. Serve hot.

Hasselback Potatoes with Chive Pesto

Prep time: 10 minutes | Cook time: 40 minutes | Serves 2

- 2 medium Maris Piper potatoes
- 5 tablespoons olive oil
- coarse sea salt and freshly ground black pepper, to taste
- 10 g roughly chopped fresh chives
- 2 tablespoons packed fresh flat-leaf parsley leaves
- 1 tablespoon chopped walnuts
- 1 tablespoon grated Parmesan cheese
- 1 teaspoon fresh lemon juice
- 1 small garlic clove, peeled
- 60 g sour cream

1. Place the potatoes on a cutting board and lay a chopstick or thin-handled wooden spoon to the side of each potato. Thinly slice the potatoes crosswise, letting the chopstick or spoon handle stop the blade of your knife, and stop ½ inch short of each end of the potato. Rub the potatoes with 1 tablespoon of the olive oil and season with salt and pepper. 2. Place the potatoes, cut-side up, in the air fryer and air fry at 190ºC until golden brown and crisp on the outside and tender inside, about 40 minutes, drizzling the insides with 1 tablespoon more olive oil and seasoning with more salt and pepper halfway through. 3. Meanwhile, in a small blender or food processor, combine the remaining 3 tablespoons olive oil, the chives, parsley, walnuts, Parmesan, lemon juice, and garlic and purée until smooth. Season the chive pesto with salt and pepper. 4. Remove the potatoes from the air fryer and transfer to plates. Drizzle the potatoes with the pesto, letting it drip down into the grooves, then dollop each with sour cream and serve hot.

Easy Rosemary Runner Beans

Prep time: 5 minutes | Cook time: 5 minutes | Serves 1

- 1 tablespoon butter, melted
- 2 tablespoons rosemary
- ½ teaspoon salt
- 3 cloves garlic, minced
- 95 g chopped runner beans

1. Preheat the air fryer to 200ºC. 2. Combine the melted butter with the rosemary, salt, and minced garlic. Toss in the runner beans, coating them well. 3. Air fry for 5 minutes. 4. Serve immediately.

Chermoula-Roasted Beetroots

Prep time: 15 minutes | Cook time: 25 minutes | Serves 4

- Chermoula:
- 30 g packed fresh coriander leaves
- 15 g packed fresh parsley leaves
- 6 cloves garlic, peeled
- 2 teaspoons smoked paprika
- 2 teaspoons ground cumin
- 1 teaspoon ground coriander
- ½ to 1 teaspoon cayenne pepper
- Pinch crushed saffron (optional)
- 115 g extra-virgin olive oil
- coarse sea salt, to taste
- Beetroots:
- 3 medium beetroots, trimmed, peeled, and cut into 1-inch chunks
- 2 tablespoons chopped fresh coriander
- 2 tablespoons chopped fresh parsley

1. For the chermoula: In a food processor, combine the fresh

coriander, parsley, garlic, paprika, cumin, ground coriander, and cayenne. Pulse until coarsely chopped. Add the saffron, if using, and process until combined. With the food processor running, slowly add the olive oil in a steady stream; process until the sauce is uniform. Season to taste with salt. 2. For the beetroots: In a large bowl, drizzle the beetroots with ½ cup of the chermoula, or enough to coat. Arrange the beetroots in the air fryer basket. Set the air fryer to 190°C for 25 to minutes, or until the beetroots are tender. 3. Transfer the beetroots to a serving platter. Sprinkle with chopped coriander and parsley and serve.

Spiced Honey-Walnut Carrots

Prep time: 5 minutes | Cook time: 12 minutes | Serves 6

- 450 g baby carrots
- 2 tablespoons olive oil
- 80 g raw honey
- ¼ teaspoon ground cinnamon
- 25 g black walnuts, chopped

1. Preheat the air fryer to 180°C. 2. In a large bowl, toss the baby carrots with olive oil, honey, and cinnamon until well coated. 3. Pour into the air fryer and roast for 6 minutes. Shake the basket, sprinkle the walnuts on top, and roast for 6 minutes more. 4. Remove the carrots from the air fryer and serve.

Garlicky Zoodles

Prep time: 10 minutes | Cook time: 10 minutes | Serves 4

- 2 large courgette, peeled and spiralized
- 2 large yellow butternut squash, peeled and spiralized
- 1 tablespoon olive oil, divided
- ½ teaspoon rock salt
- 1 garlic clove, whole
- 2 tablespoons fresh basil, chopped
- Cooking spray

1. Preheat the air fryer to 180°C 2.Spritz the air fryer basket with cooking spray 3.Combine the courgette and butternut squash with 1 teaspoon olive oil and salt in a large bowl 4.Toss to coat well 5.Transfer the courgette and butternut squash in the preheated air fryer and add the garlic 6.Air fry for 10 minutes or until tender and fragrant 7.Toss the spiralized courgette and butternut squash halfway through the cooking time 8.Transfer the cooked courgette and butternut squash onto a plate and set aside 9.Remove the garlic from the air fryer and allow to cool for a few minutes 10.Mince the garlic and combine with remaining olive oil in a small bowl 11.Stir to mix well 12.Drizzle the spiralized courgette and butternut squash with garlic oil and sprinkle with basil 13.Toss to serve.

Simple Air Fried Crispy Brussels Sprouts

Prep time: 5 minutes | Cook time: 20 minutes | Serves 4

- ¼ teaspoon salt
- ⅛ teaspoon ground black pepper
- 1 tablespoon extra-virgin olive oil
- 450 g Brussels sprouts, trimmed and halved
- Lemon wedges, for garnish

1. Preheat the air fryer to 180°C 2.Combine the salt, black pepper, and olive oil in a large bowl 3.Stir to mix well 4.Add the Brussels sprouts to the bowl of mixture and toss to coat well 5.Arrange the Brussels sprouts in the preheated air fryer 6.Air fry for 20 minutes or until lightly browned and wilted 7.Shake the basket two times during the air frying 8.Transfer the cooked Brussels sprouts to a large plate and squeeze the lemon wedges on top to serve.

Banger-Stuffed Mushroom Caps

Prep time: 10 minutes | Cook time: 8 minutes | Serves 2

- 6 large portobello mushroom caps
- 230 g Italian banger
- 15 g chopped onion
- 2 tablespoons blanched finely ground almond flour
- 20 g grated Parmesan cheese
- 1 teaspoon minced fresh garlic

1. Use a spoon to hollow out each mushroom cap, reserving scrapings. 2. In a medium frying pan over medium heat, brown the banger about 10 minutes or until fully cooked and no pink remains. Drain and then add reserved mushroom scrapings, onion, almond flour, Parmesan, and garlic. Gently fold ingredients together and continue cooking an additional minute, then remove from heat. 3. Evenly spoon the mixture into mushroom caps and place the caps into a 6-inch round pan. Place pan into the air fryer basket. 4. Adjust the temperature to 190°C and set the timer for 8 minutes. 5. When finished cooking, the tops will be browned and bubbling. Serve warm.

Cabbage Wedges with Caraway Butter

Prep time: 30 minutes | Cook time: 35 to 40 minutes | Serves 6

- 1 tablespoon caraway seeds
- 110 g unsalted butter, at room temperature
- ½ teaspoon grated lemon zest
- 1 small head green or red cabbage, cut into 6 wedges
- 1 tablespoon avocado oil
- ½ teaspoon sea salt
- ¼ teaspoon freshly ground black pepper

1. Place the caraway seeds in a small dry frying pan over medium-high heat. Toast the seeds for 2 to 3 minutes, then remove them from the heat and let cool. Lightly crush the seeds using a mortar and pestle or with the back of a knife. 2. Place the butter in a small bowl and stir in the crushed caraway seeds and lemon zest. Form the butter into a log and wrap it in parchment paper or cling film. Refrigerate for at least 1 hour or freeze for 20 minutes. 3. Brush or spray the cabbage wedges with the avocado oil, and sprinkle with the salt and pepper. 4. Set the air fryer to190°C. Place the cabbage in a single layer in the air fryer basket and roast for 20 minutes. Flip and cook for 15 to 20 minutes more, until the cabbage is tender and lightly charred. Plate the cabbage and dot with caraway butter. Tent with foil for 5 minutes to melt the butter, and serve.

Broccoli Tots

Prep time: 15 minutes | Cook time: 10 minutes | Makes 24 tots

- 230 g broccoli florets
- 1 egg, beaten
- ⅛ teaspoon onion powder
- ¼ teaspoon salt
- ⅛ teaspoon pepper
- 2 tablespoons grated Parmesan cheese
- 25 g panko bread crumbs
- Oil for misting

1. Steam broccoli for 2 minutes. Rinse in cold water, drain well, and chop finely. 2. In a large bowl, mix broccoli with all other ingredients except the oil. 3. Scoop out small portions of mixture and shape into 24 tots. Lay them on a baking sheet or wax paper as you work. 4. Spray tots with oil and place in air fryer basket in single layer. 5. Air fry at 200°C for 5 minutes. Shake basket and spray with oil again. Cook 5 minutes longer or until browned and crispy.

Cheddar Broccoli with Bacon

Prep time: 10 minutes | Cook time: 10 minutes | Serves 2

- 215 g fresh broccoli florets
- 1 tablespoon coconut oil
- 115 g shredded sharp Cheddar cheese
- 60 g full-fat sour cream
- 4 slices sugar-free bacon, cooked and crumbled
- 1 spring onion, sliced on the bias

1. Place broccoli into the air fryer basket and drizzle it with coconut oil. 2. Adjust the temperature to 180°C and set the timer for 10 minutes. 3. Toss the basket two or three times during cooking to avoid burned spots. 4. When broccoli begins to crisp at ends, remove from fryer. Top with shredded cheese, sour cream, and crumbled bacon and garnish with spring onion slices.

Tamarind Sweet Potatoes

Prep time: 5 minutes | Cook time: 20 to 25 minutes | Serves 4

- 5 garnet sweet potatoes, peeled and diced
- 1½ tablespoons fresh lime juice
- 1 tablespoon butter, melted
- 2 teaspoons tamarind paste
- 1½ teaspoon ground allspice
- ⅓ teaspoon white pepper
- ½ teaspoon turmeric powder
- A few drops liquid stevia

1. Preheat the air fryer to 200°C. 2. In a large mixing bowl, combine all the ingredients and toss until the sweet potatoes are evenly coated. 3. Place the sweet potatoes in the air fryer basket and air fry for 20 to 25 minutes, or until the potatoes are crispy on the outside and soft on the inside. Shake the basket twice during cooking. 4. Let the potatoes cool for 5 minutes before serving.

Cauliflower Rice Balls

Prep time: 10 minutes | Cook time: 8 minutes | Serves 4

- 1 (280 g) steamer bag cauliflower rice, cooked according to package instructions
- 110 g shredded Mozzarella cheese
- 1 large egg
- 60 g plain pork scratchings, finely crushed

- ¼ teaspoon salt
- ½ teaspoon Italian seasoning

1. Place cauliflower into a large bowl and mix with Mozzarella. 2. Whisk egg in a separate medium bowl. Place pork scratchings into another large bowl with salt and Italian seasoning. 3. Separate cauliflower mixture into four equal sections and form each into a ball. Carefully dip a ball into whisked egg, then roll in pork scratchings. Repeat with remaining balls. 4. Place cauliflower balls into ungreased air fryer basket. Adjust the temperature to 200°C and air fry for 8 minutes. Rice balls will be golden when done. 5. Use a spatula to carefully move cauliflower balls to a large dish for serving. Serve warm.

Mashed Sweet Potato Tots

Prep time: 10 minutes | Cook time: 12 to 13 minutes per batch | Makes 18 to 24 tots

- 210 g cooked mashed sweet potatoes
- 1 egg white, beaten
- ⅛ teaspoon ground cinnamon
- 1 dash nutmeg
- 2 tablespoons chopped pecans
- 1½ teaspoons honey
- Salt, to taste
- 50 g panko bread crumbs
- Oil for misting or cooking spray

1. Preheat the air fryer to 200°C. 2. In a large bowl, mix together the potatoes, egg white, cinnamon, nutmeg, pecans, honey, and salt to taste. 3. Place panko crumbs on a sheet of wax paper. 4. For each tot, use about 2 teaspoons of sweet potato mixture. To shape, drop the measure of potato mixture onto panko crumbs and push crumbs up and around potatoes to coat edges. Then turn tot over to coat other side with crumbs. 5. Mist tots with oil or cooking spray and place in air fryer basket in single layer. 6. Air fry at 200°C for 12 to 13 minutes, until browned and crispy. 7. Repeat steps 5 and 6 to cook remaining tots.

Maize Croquettes

Prep time: 10 minutes | Cook time: 12 to 14 minutes | Serves 4

- 105 g leftover mashed potatoes
- 340 g maize kernels (if frozen, thawed, and well drained)
- ¼ teaspoon onion powder
- ⅛ teaspoon ground black pepper
- ¼ teaspoon salt
- 50 g panko bread crumbs
- Oil for misting or cooking spray

1. Place the potatoes and half the maize in food processor and pulse until maize is well chopped. 2. Transfer mixture to large bowl and stir in remaining maize, onion powder, pepper and salt. 3. Shape mixture into 16 balls. 4. Roll balls in panko crumbs, mist with oil or cooking spray, and place in air fryer basket. 5. Air fry at 180°C for 12 to 14 minutes, until golden brown and crispy.

Sweet and Crispy Roasted Pearl Onions

Prep time: 5 minutes | Cook time: 18 minutes | Serves 3

- 1 (410 g) package frozen pearl onions (do not thaw)
- 2 tablespoons extra-virgin olive oil
- 2 tablespoons balsamic vinegar
- 2 teaspoons finely chopped fresh rosemary
- ½ teaspoon coarse sea salt
- ¼ teaspoon black pepper

1. In a medium bowl, combine the onions, olive oil, vinegar, rosemary, salt, and pepper until well coated. 2. Transfer the onions to the air fryer basket. Set the air fryer to 200°C for 18 minutes, or until the onions are tender and lightly charred, stirring once or twice during the cooking time.

Chiles Rellenos with Red Chile Sauce

Prep time: 20 minutes | Cook time: 20 minutes | Serves 2

- Peppers:
- 2 poblano peppers, rinsed and dried
- 110 g thawed frozen or drained canned maize kernels
- 1 spring onion, sliced
- 2 tablespoons chopped fresh coriander
- ½ teaspoon coarse sea salt
- ¼ teaspoon black pepper
- 150 g grated Monterey Jack cheese
- Sauce:
- 3 tablespoons extra-virgin olive oil
- 25 g finely chopped brown onion
- 2 teaspoons minced garlic
- 1 (170 g) tin tomato paste
- 2 tablespoons ancho chilli powder

- 1 teaspoon dried oregano
- 1 teaspoon ground cumin
- ½ teaspoon coarse sea salt
- 470 ml chicken stock
- 2 tablespoons fresh lemon juice
- Mexican crema or sour cream, for serving

1. For the peppers: Place the peppers in the air fryer basket. Set the air fryer to 200°C for 10 minutes, turning the peppers halfway through the cooking time, until their skins are charred. Transfer the peppers to a resealable plastic bag, seal, and set aside to steam for 5 minutes. Peel the peppers and discard the skins. Cut a slit down the centre of each pepper, starting at the stem and continuing to the tip. Remove the seeds, being careful not to tear the chilli. 2. In a medium bowl, combine the maize, spring onion, coriander, salt, black pepper, and cheese; set aside. 3. Meanwhile, for the sauce: In a large frying pan, heat the olive oil over medium-high heat. Add the onion and cook, stirring, until tender, about 5 minutes. Add the garlic and cook, stirring, for 30 seconds. Stir in the tomato paste, chilli powder, oregano, and cumin, and salt. Cook, stirring, for 1 minute. Whisk in the stock and lemon juice. Bring to a simmer and cook, stirring occasionally, while the stuffed peppers finish cooking. 4. Cut a slit down the centre of each poblano pepper, starting at the stem and continuing to the tip. Remove the seeds, being careful not to tear the chilli. 5. Carefully stuff each pepper with half the maize mixture. Place the stuffed peppers in a baking pan. Place the pan in the air fryer basket. Set the air fryer to 200°C for 10 minutes, or until the cheese has melted. 6. Transfer the stuffed peppers to a serving platter and drizzle with the sauce and some crema.

Cauliflower Steaks Gratin

Prep time: 10 minutes | Cook time: 13 minutes | Serves 2

- 1 head cauliflower
- 1 tablespoon olive oil
- Salt and freshly ground black pepper, to taste
- ½ teaspoon chopped fresh thyme leaves
- 3 tablespoons grated Parmigiano-Reggiano cheese
- 2 tablespoons panko bread crumbs

1. Preheat the air fryer to 190°C. 2. Cut two steaks out of the centre of the cauliflower. To do this, cut the cauliflower in half and then cut one slice about 1-inch thick off each half. The rest of the cauliflower will fall apart into florets, which you tin roast on their own or save for another meal. 3. Brush both sides of the cauliflower steaks with olive oil and season with salt, freshly ground black pepper and fresh thyme. Place the cauliflower steaks into the air fryer basket and air fry for 6 minutes. Turn the steaks over and air fry for another 4 minutes. Combine the Parmesan cheese and panko bread crumbs and sprinkle the mixture over the tops of both steaks and air fry for another 3 minutes until the cheese has melted and the bread crumbs have browned. Serve this with some sautéed bitter greens and air-fried blistered tomatoes.

Breaded Green Tomatoes

Prep time: 15 minutes | Cook time: 30 minutes | Serves 4

- 60 g plain flour
- 2 eggs
- 60 g semolina
- 60 g panko bread crumbs
- 1 teaspoon garlic powder
- Salt and freshly ground black pepper, to taste
- 2 green tomatoes, cut into ½-inch-thick rounds
- Cooking oil spray

1. Place the flour in a small bowl. 2. In another small bowl, beat the eggs. 3. In a third small bowl, stir together the semolina, panko, and garlic powder. Season with salt and pepper. 4. Dip each tomato slice into the flour, the egg, and finally the semolina mixture to coat. 5. Insert the crisper plate into the basket and the basket into the unit. Preheat the unit by selecting AIR FRY, setting the temperature to 200°C, and setting the time to 3 minutes. Select START/STOP to begin. 6. Once the unit is preheated, spray the crisper plate and the basket with cooking oil. Working in batches, place the tomato slices in the air fryer in a single layer. Do not stack them. Spray the tomato slices with the cooking oil. 7. Select AIR FRY, set the temperature to 200°C, and set the time to 10 minutes. Select START/STOP to begin. 8. After 5 minutes, use tongs to flip the tomatoes. Resume cooking for 4 to 5 minutes, or until crisp. 9. When the cooking is complete, transfer the fried green tomatoes to a plate. Repeat steps 6, 7, and 8 for the remaining tomatoes.

CHAPTER 8 Vegetarian Mains

Three-Cheese Courgette Boats

Prep time: 15 minutes | Cook time: 20 minutes | Serves 2

- 2 medium courgette
- 1 tablespoon avocado oil
- 60 ml low-carb, no-sugar-added pasta sauce
- 60 g full-fat ricotta cheese
- 60 g shredded Mozzarella cheese
- ¼ teaspoon dried oregano
- ¼ teaspoon garlic powder
- ½ teaspoon dried parsley
- 2 tablespoons grated vegetarian Parmesan cheese

1. Cut off 1 inch from the top and bottom of each courgette. 2.Slice courgette in half lengthwise and use a spoon to scoop out a bit of the inside, making room for filling. 3.Brush with oil and spoon 2 tablespoons pasta sauce into each shell. In a medium bowl, mix ricotta, Mozzarella, oregano, garlic powder, and parsley. 4.Spoon the mixture into each courgette shell. Place stuffed courgette shells into the air fryer basket. 5.Adjust the temperature to 180°C and air fry for 20 minutes. To remove from the basket, use tongs or a spatula and carefully lift out. 6.Top with Parmesan. 7.Serve immediately.

Basmati Risotto

Prep time: 10 minutes | Cook time: 30 minutes | Serves 2

- 1 onion, diced
- 1 small carrot, diced
- 475 ml vegetable broth, boiling
- 120 g grated Cheddar cheese
- 1 clove garlic, minced
- 180 g long-grain basmati rice
- 1 tablespoon olive oil
- 1 tablespoon unsalted butter

1. Preheat the air fryer to 200°C. 2.Grease a baking tin with oil and stir in the butter, garlic, carrot, and onion. 3.Put the tin in the air fryer and bake for 4 minutes. 4.Pour in the rice and bake for a further 4 minutes, stirring three times throughout the baking time. 5.Turn the temperature down to 160°C. 6.Add the vegetable broth and give the dish a gentle stir. 7.Bake for 22 minutes, leaving the air fryer uncovered. 8.Pour in the cheese, stir once more and serve.

Spinach-Artichoke Stuffed Mushrooms

Prep time: 10 minutes | Cook time: 10 to 14 minutes | Serves 4

- 2 tablespoons olive oil
- 4 large portobello mushrooms, stems removed and gills scraped out
- ½ teaspoon salt
- ¼ teaspoon freshly ground pepper
- 110 g goat cheese, crumbled
- 120 g chopped marinated artichoke hearts
- 235 g frozen spinach, thawed and squeezed dry
- 120 g grated Parmesan cheese
- 2 tablespoons chopped fresh parsley

1. Preheat the air fryer to 200°C. 2.Rub the olive oil over the portobello mushrooms until thoroughly coated. 3.Sprinkle both sides with the salt and black pepper. 4.Place top-side down on a clean work surface. 5.In a small bowl, combine the goat cheese, artichoke hearts, and spinach. 6.Mash with the back of a fork until thoroughly combined. 7.Divide the cheese mixture among the mushrooms and sprinkle with the Parmesan cheese. 8.Air fry for 10 to 14 minutes until the mushrooms are tender and the cheese has begun to brown. 9.Top with the fresh parsley just before serving.

Teriyaki Cauliflower

Prep time: 5 minutes | Cook time: 14 minutes | Serves 4

- 120 ml soy sauce
- 80 ml water
- 1 tablespoon brown sugar
- 1 teaspoon sesame oil
- 1 teaspoon cornflour
- 2 cloves garlic, chopped
- ½ teaspoon chilli powder
- 1 big cauliflower head, cut into florets

1. Preheat the air fryer to 170°C. 2.Make the teriyaki sauce: In a small bowl, whisk together the soy sauce, water, brown sugar, sesame oil, cornflour, garlic, and chilli powder until well

combined. 3.Place the cauliflower florets in a large bowl and drizzle the top with the prepared teriyaki sauce and toss to coat well. 4.Put the cauliflower florets in the air fryer basket and air fry for 14 minutes, shaking the basket halfway through, or until the cauliflower is crisp-tender. 5.Let the cauliflower cool for 5 minutes before serving.

Aubergine Parmesan

Prep time: 15 minutes | Cook time: 17 minutes | Serves 4

- 1 medium aubergine, ends trimmed, sliced into ½-inch rounds
- ¼ teaspoon salt
- 2 tablespoons coconut oil
- 120 g grated Parmesan cheese
- 30 g cheese crisps, finely crushed
- 120 ml low-carb marinara sauce
- 120 g shredded Mozzarella cheese

1. Sprinkle aubergine rounds with salt on both sides and wrap in a kitchen towel for 30 minutes. 2.Press to remove excess water, then drizzle rounds with coconut oil on both sides. 3.In a medium bowl, mix Parmesan and cheese crisps. 4.Press each aubergine slice into mixture to coat both sides. 5.Place rounds into ungreased air fryer basket. 6.Adjust the temperature to 180°C and air fry for 15 minutes, turning rounds halfway through cooking. 7.They will be crispy around the edges when done. 8.Spoon marinara over rounds and sprinkle with Mozzarella. 9.Continue cooking an additional 2 minutes at 180°C until cheese is melted. 10.Serve warm.

Buckwheat Bake with Root Vegetables

Prep time: 15 minutes | Cook time: 30 minutes | Serves 6

- Olive oil cooking spray
- 2 large potatoes, cubed
- 2 carrots, sliced
- 1 small swede, cubed
- 2 celery stalks, chopped
- ½ teaspoon smoked paprika
- 60 ml plus 1 tablespoon olive oil, divided
- 2 rosemary sprigs
- 235 ml buckwheat groats
- 475 ml vegetable broth
- 2 garlic cloves, minced
- ½ brown onion, chopped
- 1 teaspoon salt

1. Preheat the air fryer to 192°C. 2. Lightly coat the inside of a 1.2 L capacity casserole dish with olive oil cooking spray. (The shape of the casserole dish will depend upon the size of the air fryer, but it needs to be able to hold at least 1.2 L.) 3. In a large bowl, toss the potatoes, carrots, swede, and celery with the paprika and 60 ml olive oil. 4. Pour the vegetable mixture into the prepared casserole dish and top with the rosemary sprigs. 5. Place the casserole dish into the air fryer and bake for 15 minutes. 6. While the vegetables are cooking, rinse and drain the buckwheat groats. 7. In a medium saucepan over medium-high heat, combine the groats, vegetable broth, garlic, onion, and salt with the remaining 1 tablespoon olive oil. 8. Bring the mixture to a boil, then reduce the heat to low, cover, and cook for 10 to 12 minutes. 9. Remove the casserole dish from the air fryer. 10. Remove the rosemary sprigs and discard. 11. Pour the cooked buckwheat into the dish with the vegetables and stir to combine. 12. Cover with aluminium foil and bake for an additional 15 minutes. 13. Stir before serving.

Mediterranean Pan Pizza

Prep time: 5 minutes | Cook time: 8 minutes | Serves 2

- 235 g shredded Mozzarella cheese
- ¼ medium red pepper, seeded and chopped
- 120 g chopped fresh spinach leaves
- 2 tablespoons chopped black olives
- 2 tablespoons crumbled feta cheese

1. Sprinkle Mozzarella into an ungreased round non-stick baking dish in an even layer. 2.Add remaining ingredients on top. 3.Place dish into air fryer basket. 4.Adjust the temperature to 180°C and bake for 8 minutes, checking halfway through to avoid burning. 5.Top of pizza will be golden brown, and the cheese melted when done. 6.Remove dish from fryer and let cool 5 minutes before slicing and serving.

Baked Farro Risotto with Sage

Prep time: 5 minutes | Cook time: 35 minutes | Serves 6

- Olive oil cooking spray
- 350 ml uncooked farro, emmer wheat or quinoa
- 600 ml chicken broth
- 235 ml tomato sauce
- 1 brown onion, diced
- 3 garlic cloves, minced
- 1 tablespoon fresh sage, chopped

- ½ teaspoon salt
- 2 tablespoons olive oil
- 235 ml Parmesan cheese, grated, divided

1. Preheat the air fryer to 192°C. 2. Lightly coat the inside of a 1.2 L capacity casserole dish with olive oil cooking spray. (The shape of the casserole dish will depend upon the size of the air fryer, but it needs to be able to hold at least 1.2 L.) 3. In a large bowl, combine the farro, broth, tomato sauce, onion, garlic, sage, salt, olive oil, and 120 ml of the Parmesan. 4. Pour the farro mixture into the prepared casserole dish and cover with aluminium foil. 5. Bake for 20 minutes, then uncover and stir. 6. Sprinkle the remaining 120 ml Parmesan over the top and bake for 15 minutes more. 7. Stir well before serving.

Garlic White Courgette Rolls

Prep time: 20 minutes | Cook time: 20 minutes | Serves 4

- 2 medium courgette
- 2 tablespoons unsalted butter
- ¼ white onion, peeled and diced
- ½ teaspoon finely minced roasted garlic
- 60 ml double cream
- 2 tablespoons vegetable broth
- ⅛ teaspoon xanthan gum
- 120 g full-fat ricotta cheese
- ¼ teaspoon salt
- ½ teaspoon garlic powder
- ¼ teaspoon dried oregano
- 475 g spinach, chopped
- 120 g sliced baby portobello mushrooms
- 180 g shredded Mozzarella cheese, divided

1. Using a mandoline or sharp knife, slice courgette into long strips lengthwise. 2.Place strips between paper towels to absorb moisture. 3.Set aside. 4.In a medium saucepan over medium heat, melt butter. 5.Add onion and sauté until fragrant. 6.Add garlic and sauté 30 seconds. 7.Pour in double cream, broth, and xanthan gum. 8.Turn off heat and whisk mixture until it begins to thicken, about 3 minutes. 9.In a medium bowl, add ricotta, salt, garlic powder, and oregano and mix well. 10.Fold in spinach, mushrooms, and 120 ml Mozzarella. 11.Pour half of the sauce into a round baking pan. 12.To assemble the rolls, place two strips of courgette on a work surface. 13.Spoon 2 tablespoons of ricotta mixture onto the slices and roll up. 14.Place seam side down on top of sauce. 15.Repeat with remaining ingredients. 16.Pour remaining sauce over the rolls and sprinkle with remaining Mozzarella. 17.Cover with foil and place into the air fryer basket. 18.Adjust the temperature to 180°C and bake for 20 minutes. 19.In the last 5 minutes, remove the foil to brown the cheese. 20.Serve immediately.

Vegetable Burgers

Prep time: 10 minutes | Cook time: 12 minutes | Serves 4

- 227 g cremini or chestnut mushrooms
- 2 large egg yolks
- ½ medium courgette, trimmed and chopped
- 60 g peeled and chopped brown onion
- 1 clove garlic, peeled and finely minced
- ½ teaspoon salt
- ¼ teaspoon ground black pepper

1. Place all ingredients into a food processor and pulse twenty times until finely chopped and combined. 2.Separate mixture into four equal sections and press each into a burger shape. 3.Place burgers into ungreased air fryer basket. 4.Adjust the temperature to 190°C and air fry for 12 minutes, turning burgers halfway through cooking. 5.Burgers will be browned and firm when done. 6.Place burgers on a large plate and let cool 5 minutes before serving.

CHAPTER 9 Treats and Desserts

Orange Gooey Butter Cake

Prep time: 5 minutes | Cook time: 1 hour 25 minutes | Serves 6 to 8

- Crust Layer:
- 30 g Plain flour
- 40 g granulated sugar
- ½ teaspoon baking powder
- ⅛ teaspoon salt
- 60 g unsalted butter, melted
- 1 egg
- 1 teaspoon orange extract
- 2 tablespoons orange zest
- Gooey Butter Layer:
- 230 g cream cheese, softened
- 110 g unsalted butter, melted
- 2 eggs
- 2 teaspoons orange extract
- 2 tablespoons orange zest
- 300 g icing sugar
- Garnish:
- Icing sugar
- Orange slices

1. Preheat the air fryer to 180°C. 2. Grease a cake pan and line the bottom with baking paper. Combine the flour, sugar, baking powder and salt in a bowl. Add the melted butter, egg, orange extract and orange zest. Mix well and press this mixture into the bottom of the greased cake pan. Lower the pan into the basket using an aluminium foil sling (fold a piece of aluminium foil into a strip about 2-inches wide by 24-inches long). Fold the ends of the aluminium foil over the top of the dish before returning the basket to the air fryer. Air fry uncovered for 8 minutes. 3. Make the gooey butter layer: Beat the cream cheese, melted butter, eggs, orange extract and orange zest in a large bowl using an electric hand mixer. Add the icing sugar in stages, beat until smooth with each addition. Pour this mixture on top of the baked crust in the cake pan. Wrap the pan with a piece of greased aluminium foil, tenting the top of the foil to leave a little room for the cake to rise. 4. Air fry for 60 minutes. Remove the aluminium foil and air fry for an additional 17 minutes. 5. Let the cake cool inside the pan for at least 10 minutes. Then, run a butter knife around the cake and let the cake cool completely in the pan. When cooled, run the butter knife around the edges of the cake again and invert it onto a plate and then back onto a serving platter. Sprinkle the icing sugar over the top of the cake and garnish with orange slices.

Cinnamon-Sugar Almonds

Prep time: 5 minutes | Cook time: 8 minutes | Serves 4

- 150 g whole almonds
- 2 tablespoons salted butter, melted
- 1 tablespoon granulated sugar
- ½ teaspoon ground cinnamon

1. In a medium bowl, combine the almonds, butter, sugar, and cinnamon. Mix well to ensure all the almonds are coated with the spiced butter. 2. Transfer the almonds to the air fryer basket and shake so they are in a single layer. Set the air fryer to 150°C, and cook for 8 minutes, stirring the almonds halfway through the cooking time. 3. Let cool completely before serving.

Eggless Farina Cake

Prep time: 30 minutes | Cook time: 25 minutes | Serves 6

- Vegetable oil
- 470 ml hot water
- 165 g chopped dried fruit, such as apricots, golden raisins, figs, and/or dates
- 165 g very fine semolina
- 235 ml milk
- 160 g granulated sugar
- 55 g ghee, butter or coconut oil, melted
- 2 tablespoons plain Greek yoghurt, or sour cream
- 1 teaspoon ground cardamom
- 1 teaspoon baking powder
- ½ teaspoon baking soda
- Whipped cream, for serving

1. Grease a baking pan with vegetable oil. 2. In a small bowl, combine the hot water and dried fruit; set aside for 20 minutes to plump up the fruit. 3. Meanwhile, in a large bowl, whisk together the semolina, milk, sugar, ghee, yoghurt and cardamom. Let stand for 20 minutes to allow the semolina to

soften and absorb some of the liquid. 4. Drain the dried fruit, and gently stir it into the batter. Add the baking powder and baking soda and stir until thoroughly combined. 5. Pour the batter into the prepared pan. Set the pan in the air fryer basket. Set the air fryer to 160°C, and cook for 25 minutes, or until a toothpick inserted into the center of the cake comes out clean. 6. Let the cake cool in the pan on a wire rack for 10 minutes. Remove the cake from the pan and let cool on the rack for 20 minutes before slicing. 7. Slice and serve topped with whipped cream.

Crispy Pineapple Rings

Prep time: 5 minutes | Cook time: 6 to 8 minutes | Serves 6

- 240 ml rice milk
- 45 g Plain flour
- 120 ml water
- 25 g unsweetened flaked coconut
- 4 tablespoons granulated sugar
- ½ teaspoon baking soda
- ½ teaspoon baking powder
- ½ teaspoon vanilla essence
- ½ teaspoon ground cinnamon
- ¼ teaspoon ground star anise
- Pinch of kosher, or coarse sea salt
- 1 medium pineapple, peeled and sliced

1. Preheat the air fryer to 190°C. 2. In a large bowl, stir together all the ingredients except the pineapple. 3. Dip each pineapple slice into the batter until evenly coated. 4. Arrange the pineapple slices in the basket and air fry for 6 to 8 minutes until golden brown. 5. Remove from the basket to a plate and cool for 5 minutes before serving warm.

Cherry Pie

Prep time: 15 minutes | Cook time: 35 minutes | Serves 6

- All-purpose flour, for dusting
- 1 package of shortcrust pastry, cut in half, at room temperature
- 350 g tin cherry pie filling
- 1 egg
- 1 tablespoon water
- 1 tablespoon sugar

1. Dust a work surface with flour and place the piecrust on it. Roll out the piecrust. Invert a shallow air fryer baking pan, or your own pie dish that fits inside the air fryer basket, on top of the dough. Trim the dough around the pan, making your cut ½ inch wider than the pan itself. 2. Repeat with the second piecrust but make the cut the same size as or slightly smaller than the pan. 3. Put the larger crust in the bottom of the baking pan. Don't stretch the dough. Gently press it into the pan. 4. Spoon in enough cherry pie filling to fill the crust. Do not overfill. 5. Using a knife or pizza cutter, cut the second piecrust into 1-inch-wide strips. Weave the strips in a lattice pattern over the top of the cherry pie filling. 6. Insert the crisper plate into the basket and the basket into the unit. Preheat to 160°C. 7. In a small bowl, whisk the egg and water. Gently brush the egg wash over the top of the pie. Sprinkle with the sugar and cover the pie with aluminium foil. 8. Once the unit is preheated, place the pie into the basket. 9. Bake for 30 minutes, remove the foil and resume cooking for 3 to 5 minutes more. The finished pie should have a flaky golden-brown crust and bubbling pie filling. 10. When the cooking is complete, serve warm. Refrigerate leftovers for a few days.

Peanut Butter, Honey & Banana Toast

Prep time: 10 minutes | Cook time: 9 minutes | Serves 4

- 2 tablespoons unsalted butter, softened
- 4 slices white bread
- 4 tablespoons peanut butter
- 2 bananas, peeled and thinly sliced
- 4 tablespoons honey
- 1 teaspoon ground cinnamon

1. Spread butter on one side of each slice of bread, then peanut butter on the other side. Arrange the banana slices on top of the peanut butter sides of each slice (about 9 slices per toast). Drizzle honey on top of the banana and sprinkle with cinnamon. 2. Cut each slice in half lengthwise so that it will better fit into the air fryer basket. Arrange two pieces of bread, butter sides down, in the air fryer basket. Set the air fryer to 190°C cooking for 5 minutes. Then set the air fryer to 200°C and cook for an additional 4 minutes, or until the bananas have started to brown. Repeat with remaining slices. Serve hot.

Lime Bars

Prep time: 10 minutes | Cook time: 33 minutes | Makes 12 bars

- 140 g blanched finely ground almond flour, divided
- 40 g powdered sweetener, divided

- 4 tablespoons salted butter, melted
- 120 ml fresh lime juice
- 2 large eggs, whisked

1. In a medium bowl, mix together 110 g flour, 25 g sweetener, and butter. Press mixture into bottom of an ungreased round nonstick cake pan. 2. Place pan into air fryer basket. Adjust the temperature to 150°C and bake for 13 minutes. Crust will be brown and set in the middle when done. 3. Allow to cool in pan 10 minutes. 4. In a medium bowl, combine remaining flour, remaining sweetener, lime juice, and eggs. Pour mixture over cooled crust and return to air fryer for 20 minutes. Top will be browned and firm when done. 5. Let cool completely in pan, about 30 minutes, then chill covered in the refrigerator 1 hour. Serve chilled.

Caramelized Fruit Skewers

Prep time: 10 minutes | Cook time: 3 to 5 minutes | Serves 4

- 2 peaches, peeled, pitted, and thickly sliced
- 3 plums, halved and pitted
- 3 nectarines, halved and pitted
- 1 tablespoon honey
- ½ teaspoon ground cinnamon
- ¼ teaspoon ground allspice
- Pinch cayenne pepper
- Special Equipment:
- 8 metal skewers

1. Preheat the air fryer to 200°C. 2. Thread, alternating peaches, plums, and nectarines, onto the metal skewers that fit into the air fryer. 3. Thoroughly combine the honey, cinnamon, allspice, and cayenne in a small bowl. Brush the glaze generously over the fruit skewers. 4. Transfer the fruit skewers to the air fryer basket. You may need to cook in batches to avoid overcrowding. 5. Air fry for 3 to 5 minutes, or until the fruit is caramelized. 6. Remove from the basket and repeat with the remaining fruit skewers. 7. Let the fruit skewers rest for 5 minutes before serving.

Olive Oil Cake

Prep time: 10 minutes | Cook time: 30 minutes | Serves 8

- 60 g blanched finely ground almond flour
- 5 large eggs, whisked
- 175 ml extra-virgin olive oil
- 75 g granulated sweetener
- 1 teaspoon vanilla extract
- 1 teaspoon baking powder

1. In a large bowl, mix all ingredients. Pour batter into an ungreased round nonstick baking dish. 2. Place dish into air fryer basket. Adjust the temperature to 150°C and bake for 30 minutes. The cake will be golden on top and firm in the center when done. 3. Let cake cool in dish 30 minutes before slicing and serving.

Appendix 1: Recipe Index

Air Fried Courgette Sticks --- 15	Butter and Bacon Chicken --- 16
Air Fried Pot Stickers --- 46	Cabbage Wedges with Caraway Butter --- 50
Air Fried Spicy Olives --- 44	Calamari with Hot Sauce --- 35
Almond Catfish --- 38	Caramelized Fruit Skewers --- 58
Almond-Crusted Chicken --- 21	Cauliflower Avocado Toast --- 7
Almond-Crusted Fish --- 37	Cauliflower Rice Balls --- 50
Apple Pie Egg Rolls --- 12	Cauliflower Steaks Gratin --- 52
Asian Marinated Salmon --- 35	Cheddar Bacon Burst with Spinach --- 30
Asparagus and Pepper Strata --- 6	Cheddar Broccoli with Bacon --- 50
Aubergine Parmesan --- 54	Cheddar Eggs --- 5
Bacon and Cheese Stuffed Pork Chops --- 26	Cheesy Chilli Toast --- 14
Bacon, Egg, and Cheese Roll Ups --- 9	Cheesy Loaded Broccoli --- 47
Bacon-Wrapped Cheese Pork --- 33	Cheesy Scrambled Eggs --- 5
Bacon-Wrapped Chicken Breasts Rolls --- 17	Cheesy Steak Fries --- 43
Bacon-Wrapped Hot Dogs --- 12	Chermoula-Roasted Beetroots --- 48
Bacon-Wrapped Stuffed Chicken Breasts --- 21	Cherry Pie --- 57
Baked Farro Risotto with Sage --- 54	Chicken and Gruyère Cordon Bleu --- 18
Baked Monkfish --- 38	Chicken Fried Steak with Cream Gravy --- 31
Baked Potato Breakfast Boats --- 8	Chicken Hand Pies --- 23
Banger and Cauliflower Arancini --- 24	Chicken Strips with Satay Sauce --- 19
Banger-Stuffed Mushroom Caps --- 49	Chicken Thighs with Coriander --- 22
Barbecue Chicken Bites --- 22	Chiles Rellenos with Red Chile Sauce --- 51
Basmati Risotto --- 53	Chilli-brined Fried Calamari --- 41
Beef Burger --- 25	Chipotle Drumsticks --- 20
Beef Mince Taco Rolls --- 27	Cinnamon Rolls --- 9
Beefy Poppers --- 24	Cinnamon-Raisin Bagels --- 8
Berry Cheese cake --- 12	Cinnamon-Sugar Almonds --- 56
Blackened Cajun Chicken Tenders --- 18	Coriander Lime Chicken Thighs --- 17
Blackened Chicken --- 17	Courgette Balls --- 48
Blackened Steak Nuggets --- 27	Courgette Feta Roulades --- 41
Bourbon Vanilla Eggy Bread --- 6	Crab and Pepper Cakes --- 35
Breaded Green Tomatoes --- 52	Crispy Breaded Beef Cubes --- 44
Breakfast Cobbler --- 9	Crispy Courgette Sticks --- 47
Breakfast Pitta --- 6	Crispy Green Bean Fries with Lemon-Yoghurt Sauce --- 42
Broccoli Tots --- 50	
Bruschetta Chicken --- 20	Crispy Pineapple Rings --- 57
Buckwheat Bake with Root Vegetables --- 54	Crispy Prawns with Coriander --- 34
Bunless Breakfast Turkey Burgers --- 5	Crunchy Air Fried Cod Fillets --- 34

Recipe	Page
Crustless Prawn Quiche	38
Easy Rosemary Runner Beans	48
Easy Scallops	35
Easy Spiced Nuts	43
Eggless Farina Cake	56
Ethiopian Chicken with Cauliflower	20
Filipino Crispy Pork Belly	28
Fish Gratin	36
Five-Spice Pork Belly	24
Friday Night Fish-Fry	39
Fried Chicken Wings with Waffles	10
Fruited Gammon	32
Garlic and Thyme Tomatoes	47
Garlic Soy Chicken Thighs	22
Garlic White Courgette Rolls	55
Garlicky Zoodles	49
Goat Cheese and Garlic Crostini	44
Golden Chicken Cutlets	20
Greek Chicken Souvlaki	16
Greek Pork with Tzatziki Sauce	28
Greek Potato Skins with Olives and Feta	45
Greek Stuffed Fillet	33
Greek Yoghurt Devilled Eggs	45
Harissa-Rubbed Chicken	16
Hasselback Potatoes with Chive Pesto	48
Hearty Blueberry Porridge	11
Herb-Crusted Lamb Chops	25
Herb-Roasted Veggies	13
Homemade Toaster Pastries	10
Italian Banger Links	28
Italian Crispy Chicken	22
Italian Steak Rolls	32
Jalapeño Popper Egg Cups	10
Jalapeño Popper Pork Chops	29
Kheema Burgers	27
Lamb Burger with Feta and Olives	26
Lebanese Muhammara	44
Lemon-Basil Turkey Breasts	17
Lemon-Blueberry Muffins	6
Lemon-Dijon Boneless Chicken	18
Lime Bars	57
Maize Croquettes	51
Mashed Sweet Potato Tots	51
Mediterranean Pan Pizza	54
Mediterranean Stuffed Chicken Breasts	19
Mexican Potato Skins	41
Mixed Vegetables Pot Stickers	45
Mushroom and Green Bean Casserole	13
Not-So-English Muffins	5
Oat and Chia Porridge	11
Olive Oil Cake	58
Onion Pork Kebabs	26
Orange Gooey Butter Cake	56
Pancake for Two	6
Panko-Crusted Fish Fingers	39
Parmesan and Herb Sweet Potatoes	47
Parmesan Mackerel with Coriander	39
Parmesan-Crusted Pork Chops	32
Parmesan-Thyme Butternut Marrow	47
Peanut Butter, Honey & Banana Toast	57
Pepperoni Pizza Dip	45
Pork Burgers with Red Cabbage Salad	12
Pork Milanese	30
Pork Stuffing Meatballs	13
Portobello Eggs Benedict	8
Quesadillas	8
Ritzy Skirt Steak Fajitas	31
Roasted Mushrooms with Garlic	43
Rosemary-Garlic Shoestring Fries	42
Scalloped Veggie Mix	14
Scallops with Asparagus and Peas	36
Scotch Eggs	7
Sesame-Crusted Tuna Steak	36
Simple Air Fried Crispy Brussels Sprouts	49
Simple Beef Mince with Courgette	29
Simple Cheesy Shrimps	39
Simple Cinnamon Toasts	9
Simple Pea Delight	14
Snapper Scampi	38
Spice-Coated Steaks with Cucumber and Snap Pea Salad	30
Spiced Honey-Walnut Carrots	49
Spiced Roasted Cashews	41
Spice-Rubbed Pork Loin	27
Spinach and Bacon Roll-ups	5
Spinach and Carrot Balls	14

Spinach and Crab Meat Cups---------------------- 42	Teriyaki Cauliflower------------------------------- 53
Spinach-Artichoke Stuffed Mushrooms----------53	Tex-Mex Salmon Bowl----------------------------36
Spiralized Potato Nest with Tomato Tomato Ketchup-- 43	Three-Cheese Courgette Boats---------------------53
Steak and Vegetable Kebabs----------------------- 13	Tilapia Sandwiches with Tartar Sauce------------37
Steak Gyro Platter----------------------------------31	Tilapia with Pecans-------------------------------- 37
Sweet and Crispy Roasted Pearl Onions---------- 51	Tuna and Fruit Kebabs---------------------------- 34
Sweet and Spicy Country-Style Ribs-------------- 25	Turkish Chicken Kebabs--------------------------18
Sweet Chili Spiced Chicken------------------------21	Vegetable Burgers----------------------------------55
Sweet Maize and Carrot Fritters-------------------- 14	Vietnamese-- 29
Tamarind Sweet Potatoes--------------------------- 50	Western Frittata-------------------------------------7

Printed in Great Britain
by Amazon